MODELLING
HISTORIC BUILDINGS AND IMAGINARY STRUCTURES

A Guide for Railway Modellers and Diorama Model Makers

MODELLING
HISTORIC BUILDINGS AND IMAGINARY STRUCTURES

A Guide for Railway Modellers and Diorama Model Makers

DAVID WRIGHT

THE CROWOOD PRESS

First published in 2021 by
The Crowood Press Ltd
Ramsbury, Marlborough
Wiltshire SN8 2HR

enquiries@crowood.com

www.crowood.com

British Library Cataloguing-in-Publication Data
A catalogue record for this book is available from the British Library.

ISBN 978 1 78500 804 7

Designed and typeset by Guy Croton
Publishing Services, West Malling, Kent

Printed and bound in India by Replika Press Pvt. Ltd.

CONTENTS

DEDICATION

I would like to dedicate this, my seventh book, to a special group of people: the exhibition managers and their many helpers. This dedicated group has devoted so much of their own time and effort, for free, to stage the model railway, and other miniature-related exhibitions.

ACKNOWLEDGEMENTS

Also I would like to pass on my special thanks to the following: Kate Murphy of Sinai Park House; Leslie Smith and Gareth Williams of Tutbury Castle; Caroline Talbot of Hawkstone Park Follies; Trevor Middleton and Charlie Glenn of Codnor Castle Heritage Trust; and my wife Karen. I thank all of them for their contributions towards the production of this book.

INTRODUCTION

In this, the seventh book I have put together for Crowood, I have purposely tried to present the contents in a way that I hope will fire the modeller's imagination, rather than following exacting constraints. This will be especially evident for the model railway hobby, where for the most part modellers are trying to recreate a prototype as closely as possible down to the very last detail.

This desire for miniature perfection is especially true of the older modeller, who might be trying to create in model form what they remember from childhood. Others will try to create a three-dimensional miniature record of times before they were born, when the railways were at their peak.

These modellers will have to rely on historical records and photographs in order first to gain reference before creating their models. They would most likely have experienced the real railway when steam was king, and the railways were thought to be more attractive. This was most probably made more interesting because of the railway infrastructure evident at this time. The result of this has seen the model railway market catering for the older railway modeller, especially in recent years.

The model railway trade has therefore seen the creation of ready-to-run locomotives and rolling stock to appeal to most tastes, from pre-grouping up to the diesel era. If it is not available now 'out of the box', then there is probably a kit available, and there are many extra detailing parts for either the scratch builder or those who want to 'super detail' their 'out-of-the-box' models.

All these modellers were young in a world that was very different to the one we live in today. Life was simpler, I suppose, and for any young boy in the 1950s trainspotting and fishing were the main pastimes for this young generation. This was also true of the next generation growing up in the 1960s and 1970s, although steam had given way to diesel by this time, and popular music was, of course, a big influence on the young.

However, the modern world of today has changed dramatically, especially with the ever-growing advances in technology. The young of today are bombarded with immediate communications, instant gaming, and a vast number of images readily available at a touch of the screen on a smartphone, tablet or laptop computer. The younger generation have therefore mainly turned their back on any creative hands-on hobbies and pastimes, which tend to be considered as not being cool any more!

This is a shame, as we need new blood to move the hobby on for the future, otherwise we will see it disappear completely. This has concerns for me, as we need to be creative with both our hands and our minds. Model making is one of the best ways to keep these skills alive. This is why I have constructed this book in a way that I hope will appeal to the younger generation as well as older modellers.

As youngsters we always have a vivid imagination, although as we grow older, for most of us the responsibilities of life start to take over, and imagination becomes lost to reality. I remember my childhood vividly, in particular not being able to look over a high wall and wondering what lay beyond. My imagination would kick in, leading me into a fantasy world that might be lying on the other side.

This imagination has stayed with some into adulthood, and these few have used it creatively to produce great works of fiction and music, as well as visually towards creating unbelievable concept art for film productions. It is this imagination I want to bring to the fore in this book, and I hope it will perhaps inspire some of the younger generation to get 'hands on' again.

The castle has always evoked interest in the young mind; this is most likely to have been obtained from imagery seen in films or childhood story books. This has possibly led to an interest carried forward to explore the real structures. This interest has recently expanded amongst some teenagers, and has developed into the three-dimensional gaming hobby. Of course this is for the most part hinged totally on fantasy, so castles will be playing a major part. When looking at this hobby in more detail I have noticed the skills involved, and some of the materials used are not dissimilar to those of the model railway hobby – and yet they seem to be totally alienated from each other.

I have therefore purposely used projects in this book that would be both attractive and in some cases recognizable to both sets of model makers; this I hope will bring the creative skills of future modellers together. One major project will be themed in this way, combining the model railway with an imaginary or fantasy setting.

We can also combine structures such as castles and follies with reality when it comes to railway modelling. I can think of a few examples where castles feature directly or close to the railway. Conwy, for instance, immediately comes to mind, along with Corfe Castle on the Swanage branch. Knaresborough is also a good

This super model diorama was constructed by the late Ray Williams of Belper, Derbyshire; it is now owned by John Huddlestone. The model is called 'Combourge', and features a fine trolley-bus layout. It is totally scratch built, using a combination of wood, styrene sheet and modelling plaster. All the stonework is hand painted and is superbly detailed and dressed out. The castle and the various shops and cottages represent the architecture of the Brittany region of France. For those interested in the trolley buses operated on the layout, they represent the following systems: Saint Maio, Limoges, Grenoble and St Étienne.

A lovely model of a European castle surrounded by a narrow-gauge railway. The whole model diorama is on its own island surrounded by water in the form of a lake, and just shows what can be achieved in a very small space.

example, with the railway passing close to the ruins of the fourteenth-century castle. This has been modelled by Pete Goss in his incredible exhibition layout 'The World's End'. The folly features on a few exhibition layouts too, such as 'Weaver Hill' by Benjamin & Richard Brady, where a number have been incorporated within the scenic part of the layout.

Follies have no direct purpose other than being situated where landowners wanted to improve a view or create a fantasy structure. Most of these structures resemble a 'sham' castle, such as the one crowning the crag at Mow Cop. This impressive structure was the creation of Randle Wilbraham in 1760. Another folly following this style is 'Old John' standing in Bradgate Park near to Leicester. It was built in 1786 by the 5th Earl of Stamford. This folly will feature later in the book as part of the 'Raven's Ravine' project.

In the books I have compiled in the past, I have strictly concentrated on British outline modelling. In this book, however, although the subjects for the projects are British based, with a little alteration and imagination they would easily fit into any continental or even worldwide outline model railway or diorama.

I hope that by selecting a more fantasy-based theme with some of the projects, this will trigger the imagination of the older generation as well, so they consider constructing a starter model railway or diorama along with their children or their grandchildren. In this way I am sure that the younger mind will be inspired again, just as it was when I built my first model railway together with my father many years ago. It is also to be hoped that this approach will bring the relationship between the generations much closer together, particularly as the distractions of the modern world have so often caused them to drift apart.

MAKING A START

Before we move on to the first chapter I want to give a brief overview of the projects contained within this book. One of the main objectives of the projects was to use either scrap or very low cost materials for their construction. After all, we don't always have large amounts of money to spend on our hobbies these days. It will also make it possible for the young modeller to create something that they can be proud of, and at the same time help towards recycling materials in today's throw-away society. Most of the projects will consist of creating historic buildings or structures either based on a prototype, or using parts of the prototype to create an imaginary model.

Even with the imaginary or fantasy models we wish to make, it is important that we have some knowledge of the reason or purpose for its existence. This can be taken a stage further by examining the materials used for its construction. So let's take a little time before we start any model making to consider this.

In this country we are blessed to have such a rich history, and an impressive number of historic buildings and structures that have survived the passing of time. For the most part we as a nation have always taken pride in our building heritage, and in most cases have ensured the preservation and upkeep of historic structures for future generations to enjoy. Our heritage has been used for numerous Hollywood feature film productions, using some of the buildings directly, or in part as backdrops.

Major organizations such as the National Trust and English Heritage, as well as a good number of other smaller heritage and conservation groups, have been responsible for their preservation and upkeep. It is these organizations that have made it possible for members of the general public to gain access to many of the properties, ruins and historic structures today.

The 'Nine Stones Close', a Bronze Age stone circle standing on Harthill Moor, near to Winster in the Derbyshire Peak District. A stone circle such as this will make an interesting feature to add to a model railway layout or a fantasy-themed diorama.

For us as modellers, these organizations can also provide further reference material, with on-site historic records available. If you are lucky, you can view photographs, drawings and plans from collections at a local museum, library or the local council records office. It's always worth contacting them, and usually they are only too happy to help. Then of course there is always the internet, with a vast amount of information available from sites such as 'Wikipedia'. You might find that a book has been published that covers the subject you wish to model. This might be available commercially, or contained in the reference section of the local studies library. I have found my local studies library invaluable in the past, especially for providing historical large-scale maps to help me with my model-making projects.

The next step is to examine the materials used for the construction of either a building or a structure. Most will be built of materials that are sourced locally. Before mass transportation this would have been the norm, although there are exceptions to this, even going right back to the Neolithic age around 3,000BC. The bluestones used for the construction of Stonehenge were transported all the way from the Preseli Hills in south-west Wales to Salisbury Plain, a distance of 250km. Even the larger sarsen stones were transported from the Marlborough Downs, some 20 miles (30km) to the site of the monument.

These ancient religious sites can always feature within a model railway, of course. A stone circle, burial chamber or a standing-stone monolith will always create a point of interest. This could be extended to standing stones contained within legends. The 'Devils' Arrows' are three such monoliths that stand near to Boroughbridge in North Yorkshire, a puzzling legacy left by prehistoric man. Then there are always the actual or imaginary structures associated with the legendary land of King Arthur.

The very first settlers in our country used naturally formed rock formations, where caves became

The man-made caves at Formark, in south Derbyshire. The caves have been given the name of 'Anchor Church', and are thought to have been carved out of the sandstone rock by a hermit. Like standing stones, it would be worth considering adding caves such as these to a model.

Caves and rock features can also accommodate interesting buildings. 'Ye Olde Trip to Jerusalem' claims – as the sign says – to be the oldest inn in England. It is built directly into the side of Castle Rock, making good use of the natural caves for extra accommodation. Today the inn is one of the main tourist attractions in the City of Nottingham.

utilized for a dwelling. Although we might think of caves being used for shelter as totally reserved to the Stone Age, this is not always the case. If the geology of the area has created naturally formed caves, then these will have been used for dwellings. In fact caves have been used for homes up until recent years, and some are still used today. The only difference is the construction of a more traditional frontage, which has been added to the cave using materials we are more familiar with. A good example of this are the Rock Houses at Kinver Edge in the south of Staffordshire, and 'Ye Old Trip to Jerusalem' public house built into the sandstone of Castle Rock in Nottingham.

In some cases the materials used for construction may have changed – for instance many of our castles originally consisted of a motte and bailey, with a ditch or moat dug into the earthworks. This would have been surrounded by a timber stockade, while inside the buildings would be timber framed with walls of wattle and daub and roofs of thatch. It was the Normans who were responsible for building castles of stronger materials. The stockade would have been replaced with a high curtain wall, broken at intervals with a defensive tower or turret, all constructed from stone to a thickness of several feet. The reason for rebuilding was to improve the castle's defences, to keep out the armies of marauding raiders.

Most of the less important buildings of this period would still have been built from traditional materials, with timber-framed construction being most commonly found throughout most parts of the British Isles. The early examples consisted of a main cruck frame, where two large, naturally formed oak curved timber beams were brought together at the apex. An extra cross-beam was added to form something like a gigantic letter 'A'. From a set of two or more main trusses, purlin timbers were positioned laterally to hold the many rafters in position.

A very early dwelling, reconstructed at St Fagan's National History Museum, near Cardiff. The single-storey dwelling is known as 'Nant Wallter Cottage', and has been built with walls of 'clom', the name given to a mixture of local clay with straw. The roof was made from layers of gorse, overlaid with a topping of straw thatch.

The remains of the south curtain wall of Codnor Castle. This section includes the ogge arched window. Castles in a state of ruin such as this can provide a very impressive visual feature to both a model railway or to a themed diorama.

On very early buildings these would have been crude, and would not have been squared off. Thinner timbers known as withies would then have been interwoven through the rafters, creating a base for the roofing material. Most likely this would have consisted of a layer of bracken or heather, as a base for the final covering of thatch. In highland or moorland areas, where straw or reed was not available, then another thick covering of heather would have been used.

Later, buildings would still use the timber frame for their main construction, though a box frame replaced the cruck frame. Many examples of this type of building can still be seen throughout the UK today. The first project model in this book features a historic building built by this method.

Where stone was readily available this would have been used for the building of cottages and other buildings of lesser importance. The next few selected projects feature buildings and structures built from stone, including the last project in the book, where I will show the modelling of structures constructed from this ubiquitous material.

When brick making became established as a mass commercial industry, many newer buildings and structures were built using this building material. Bricks of course offered not only durability, but more importantly a regular size, which made construction much easier and quicker.

More recently, concrete has been used for buildings, and many other structures. Concrete, together with the inclusion of steel rods to reinforce the material, is very tough and durable. Buildings and structures using this material can either be built on site, or prefabricated sections can be built elsewhere and then brought to the site and assembled there. The material was ideal for buildings intended for defence, and was used extensively in both World Wars.

I hope that this book and its projects will inspire you to try out some of the modelling methods and materials used. I have purposely put together one chapter to include the construction of a whole diorama, with a small model railway as the main focal point. In this diorama I have tried

A more modern defensive structure. There were thousands of pre-cast concrete pill boxes such as this, built in case of a German land invasion. A good number still remain today, including this example constructed to guard the banks of the River Dove. A structure such as this would not look out of place on any post-war model railway or military-themed diorama.

This pill-box structure is effectively located as a feature on a model railway.

This folly, topping a rocky crag overlooking the Cheshire Plain, is 'Mow Cop'. It was built simply to enhance the view from a wealthy land owner's estate. This structure, purposely built to replicate a ruined castle in appearance, would make a fascinating subject for a model.

to show how various impressive structures can be modelled from low cost materials, but also how to bring them together within a dramatic modelled terrain.

I have also provided a colour mixing guide as a special appendix in this book. When presenting demonstrations at model railway and general model shows, one thing I am always asked is how to make up and apply realistic colour. I hope that providing a guide within this book will make this task a little more understandable.

Happy model making!

DAVID WRIGHT

CHAPTER ONE

MODELLING A HISTORIC TIMBER-FRAMED BUILDING

In this country there are many examples of timber-framed buildings, especially those constructed of a timber box frame. Towns such as Lavenham in Suffolk can boast many such buildings, including the magnificent Guild Hall. All the buildings in this town were built on the wealth of the wool trade, and still survive today – so I could have chosen an existing example to model.

However, the building I decided to model no longer exists, so the benefit of an existing prototype was not an option. This choice was definitely going to be a challenge, but would create another dimension to the hobby of model making. I wanted to model a building that had a notable historical background – however, the building I had in mind had not survived the passage of time, mainly because it was not seen to be that important for the purpose for which it was originally built.

The gable over the porch to the Guildhall in the Suffolk town of Lavenham. The building is of a similar age to the lodging, so it was used as reference for style when constructing the main porch on the model.

THE PROJECT: 'MARY'S LODGING'

The building in question originated as a simple half-timbered hunting lodge located within the curtain walls of Tutbury Castle. The castle, situated overlooking the Dove Valley in East Staffordshire, was singled out as the perfect place to imprison Mary Queen of Scots on four occasions. For the first three times she was imprisoned in the South Tower, but on her fourth visit she was kept in this hunting lodge, which became known as 'Mary's lodging'. Mary was, of course, a threat to the Tudor Queen Elizabeth and the Protestant religion of England at this time in history. During her last imprisonment at Tutbury she became involved in a plot to escape and put herself on the English throne instead of the Protestant

A view of the Guildhall to show the side profile of the porch.

A preliminary sketch of how 'Mary's lodging' might have appeared in 1585. The sketch was based firstly on archaeological information found at the site, secondly on a drawing of the castle's inner bailey that appeared in papers belonging to Mary's gaoler, and thirdly from architectural reference and studies of timber-framed buildings of the same period.

An illustration of how 'Mary's lodging' was originally perceived, including my visual interpretation showing the colour of the walls and the handmade terracotta roofing tiles.

Queen Elizabeth. But this plot was discovered, and resulted in a move locally to Chartley; she was then sent to Fotheringhay Castle in Northamptonshire, where she was executed in 1586.

MAKING A START

Where do we make a start on a model of a building with no drawings or photographic reference existing? A good way to start this project was to arrange a visit to the site at Tutbury and talk with someone who might be able to give me a few clues as to how this building would have appeared. I was lucky enough to talk with a historian who had in recent years conducted several archaeological digs on the site. The information that had been collected gave evidence of the footprint, and therefore we could estimate some measurements of the building. This, together with fragments of various building materials dug from the ground, gave a reasonable starting point. There was also a rather crude plan of the inner bailey of the castle in the papers of Mary's gaoler, which illustrated her lodgings, showing the building to be long and thin with a full length gabled roof.

Another avenue open to me was to search for other buildings of this time that were constructed from similar materials. One such building was 'Sinai Park House', an impressive timber-framed manor house. Originally built as two timber houses by the monks of Burton Abbey, it was later acquired by the Paget family. The house was extended and used at this time for hunting, and was situated only 5 miles (8km) away from Tutbury. Although the extensions were later than our building, there is a good chance that the oak timbers would have been sourced from the same woodland, this being 'The Forest of Needwood', which lay only a few miles away from both buildings.

Close-up of the restored wing of 'Sinai Park House'. Although built later than 'Mary's lodging', it would have been built from similar oak timbers, sourced locally for both buildings in the nearby 'Forest of Needwood'.

The gable end of the north wing of 'Sinai Park House'. Note the scaffolding holding up the crumbling skeleton timber frame. This part of the building, as you can see, has still to be restored to its former glory.

MAKING A DRAWING AND A SCALE PLAN

My next plan was to draw up a visual impression of how the building might have looked from the information found and given to me on site at Tutbury. I also had a number of photographs taken and site drawings made when I arranged a visit to Sinai Park House; I also took a look at some of the existing buildings to be found in Lavenham. From the evidence found on site, at Tutbury, the footprint showed small extensions on the facing side. These were most likely to have been porches, and would have been similar to examples found fronting buildings of the same age in the Suffolk town.

From the drawing made and with some measurements taken of the footprint, a scale plan could be drawn up ready to start the model. This was drawn up to 1:48th or ¼in to the foot, which would give the results I was looking for with this model, and would make the best use of the materials I was going to select in the course of constructing it. I needed now to look at how the model would be constructed. After thinking this out and spending some time looking over the drawing, I came to the conclusion that the easiest way would be to make up sections of the timber frame first, including the rendered infill panels. This would also include any window or door apertures that could be readily cut out.

CHOICE OF MATERIALS

The next stage was to consider the materials from which to construct this model.

FOR THE FRAME

From the start I wanted to use actual wood for the timber frame, making the model appear more authentic. Card would be fine for the panels, which I intended to cover with a thin skin of Das modelling clay to represent the wattle-and-daub infill. The card would only be used as the facing material, as a stronger material would be needed for the main construction. After much consideration I finally opted for Foamex.

This is similar to foam board, although the centre is much more condensed as it is made up from compressed PVC. The sheets are also laminated with PVC on both sides, making the whole construction more durable and ridged than foam board. It can be obtained from exhibition suppliers, and is now used extensively in the graphics trade for exhibition or shop display panels. If you know anyone employed in this trade, it might be worth contacting them to see if you can obtain any off-cuts.

OTHER TIMBER FEATURES

For the timber mullion window frames I decided to try ordinary matchsticks, which would give a good impression at this scale. The planked door could easily be fabricated from coffee stirrers – again these are perfect for this feature in this scale. Other timber features, such as the visible jetting beams, roof rafters, barge boards and any decorative mouldings, could be obtained from dolls' house suppliers. However, the carved corner brackets fitted to support the jetted-out upper floor would have to be specially made.

FOR THE ROOF

The roof covering consists of handmade terracotta tiles, and could be made from card. I normally recommend using old greetings cards for this purpose, as cards can usually be found that are the correct thickness for your models. At the same time you will be reusing cards that will only be thrown away or go to recycling.

FOR THE LEADED WINDOWS AND GLAZING

For the leaded windows and the glazing, celluloid sheet would be the best option, with the lead strips pre-printed on. However, this was a problem, as no commercial sheets existed that fitted this description and were in the correct scale. I therefore had the option either to try to make them up by scoring the diamond leaded pattern on to the celluloid, and filling them in afterwards, or sourcing them from one of the model suppliers. I opted for the second choice, and these are now available from 'Freestone Models'.

The timber frame and the timbers forming the jetting beams to support the wider upper floor.

The first option would have worked, although I thought the pre-printed ones would have looked neater. This is because the scoring method would need to be followed by adding thinned-down oil paint over the whole of celluloid sheet, and then wiping it off again, allowing the paint to remain in the scored-out grooves. Obviously this would create a smear over the clear celluloid, and it would be very difficult to remove all the residue paint from where it was not required.

FOR THE CHIMNEYS

The only major construction item left to consider was how to form the ornate brick chimneys, and what materials to use. Four would be needed on this model, with two stacks topping each rectangular base. Wood was selected and cut square to the required scale width. The right-angled corners were then cut at forty-five degrees, creating an eight-sided octagonal profile. The sides were then carefully fluted using a concave woodworking chisel. Extra detail was then added, which I will explain during the construction methods used for this model. For this project, however, I only made up one stack simply to save time. This was used as a master, and the stacks for the model were then cast in resin.

SOURCING ANTIQUE OAK

Before we look at building the model, I would like to elaborate further on some of the timber acquired for its construction. I thought it would be appropriate if real timber were used for the framing, and furthermore antique oak dating back to the Tudor period, if it was available. To my amazement I found a supplier to the dolls' house trade that supplied cut-down strips of oak sourced from old ships dating from this period in history. I managed to purchase a number of relative widths for this model, which also came with proof of their historical provenance.

CONSTRUCTION OF THE MODEL

With all the materials that were considered suitable sourced and obtained, construction could now be addressed. I started by cutting the main corner posts and lower floor support timbers or studs to the desired length. Next the wall panels were measured out and cut to size, starting with the front wall. These were cut from the Foamex board, but I decided not to make the facing wall to full length, but to make it up from several panels consisting of shorter lengths.

The construction of the walls, with the timber frame and the infill of wattle and daub clearly visible.

A selection of tools and materials used to start this model. The materials include Foamex board and artist's mount board.

This would make handling easier, and they could be joined together later on in the construction process.

The positions for the stud upright timbers were marked on the panels, along with the window and door apertures before the latter were all cut out. The window apertures were purposely cut slightly oversize to allow the glazing to be fixed in at a later stage. The upright stud timbers could now be glued to the wall panels, following the measured out spacing.

FITTING THE FACING PANELS

The next task was to fit in the facing panels to hold the render. These were measured out and then cut

Construction has started on the lower-floor panels, showing the positioning of the timber framing on the walls. The construction began with 'Foamex', used to create a substantial backing for the model. The close stud vertical timbers and the corner posts were cut from oak dating close to those used on the original building. Mounting card was then cut to fill in between the vertical timbers before being faced with Das modelling clay. Also in view are the timber mullions fitted into position, all made from matchsticks to form the lower floor window frames.

to size before being glued in the space left between the upright stud timbers. Mounting card was used here, as it is only 1.5mm thick and so would allow for the timbers to stand slightly proud. The window apertures would be cut again, however, this time they would be cut to the actual size.

This process was repeated on all the facing panels, which were put on one side ready for the next stage. I then moved on to making up the rear lower wall and the two lower end walling panels in the same way.

Applying the Render

Once all these were at the same stage, the render could be added. This was achieved by applying a thin skin of Das modelling clay. To do this, first PVA was brushed on, then the Das was applied with wet fingers to the desired thickness. To persuade the Das to fit up to the timbers neatly I used a dentist's probe; however, a coffee stirrer will do the same job. Once Das has been added to all the panels, all the walling panels can be left for about twenty-four hours to completely dry off.

Das clay being added to recreate the daub covering. Note that a coffee stirrer has been used to push the wet clay into the joins and any tight corners.

Balsa wood has been used as an alternative to oak on the upper floor. Also note that the window frame has been made up from matchsticks to form both the vertical mullions and the horizontal transoms.

Once the clay is dry on the panels, extra work can be carried out, including scratching the surface in order to create a distressed finish such as would be typical of this unmaintained building. Next the window mullions were fixed in, using matchsticks for assembly. I decided to add finishes to the prefabricated panels so they were nearly finished and ready for final assembly.

The doors were now made up using the coffee stirrers as boards: first these were cut to length and positioned side by side, then two stretcher stiles were glued on, so as to hold the 'boards' together.

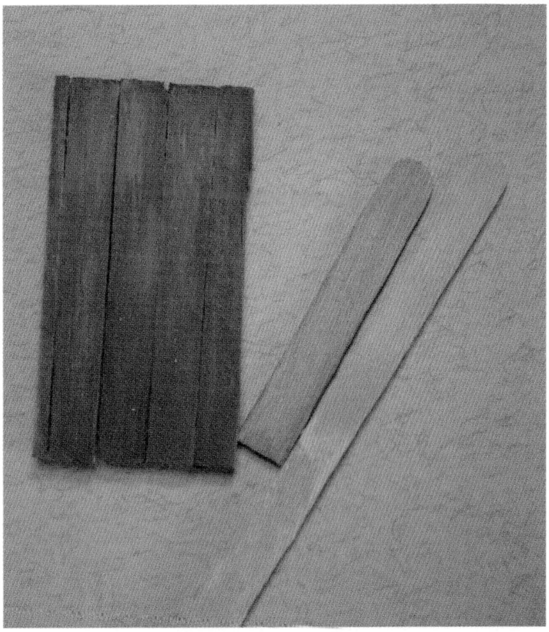

RIGHT: ***All the vertical planked doors for the lodging were made directly from coffee stirrers. It is always worth considering using these for model making, as they can be very useful.***

BELOW: ***The first planked door is fitted into the door frame. All the timbers have been painted, along with the daub-covered walling. The timberwork has been painted using artists' oil paints in a shade of mid-grey. The daub covering has been painted using a thinned-down coat of a buff colour. All the made-up panels were painted at this stage, as it is easier to reach and paint parts before final assembly. Any final touching up and weathering can be carried out once the building has been assembled.***

PAINTING THE TIMBER FEATURES AND PANELS

With all the doors and window mullion frames now fixed into position, I could paint all the timber features and the distressed rendered wattle-and-daub facing panels. The colour mix for the timber was made up from Payne's grey, a small amount of raw umber with titanium white, and a little Naples yellow added, so as to give the desired 'aged' look to the woodwork. Next the rendering was painted using Naples yellow and a little titanium white. I used artists' oil paint for both, as the oil paint reacts perfectly with the

The construction of one of the building's upper gable ends. Note that the entire timber frame has been completed, including replicating and fixing the joining pegs. The upper window frame has also been completed apart from the glazing, and all the clay infill has been applied. Finally all the painting has been finished, so this panel is nearly ready for assembly.

Das modelling clay and all the timbers used for the woodwork.

The timbers would need to be worked over with a dry mix of the titanium white, with some of this rubbed in with the fingers. This technique will give the silvered weathered look to all the timberwork, including the mullion window frames. You could also use white chalk or oil pastels to give the same results.

FIXING THE GLAZING

It was necessary to fix in the glazing of the windows while working on the flat prefabricated sections. I cut the pre-printed celluloid sheets to fit inside the frame, selecting the diamond pattern so that it also fitted within the visible area of the window. The cut-out pieces of glazing were then secured to the inside of the frames using an impact adhesive, making sure that none ended up on the face of the celluloid.

Adding the Jetting Beams

Before moving on to the assembly of the upper floor, the jetting beams need to be added to the top beams of the lower ground section. These were cut to length from 3 x 3mm square-cut timber and glued into position, each being spaced about 10mm apart, with extra pieces of the same timber fitted into the spaces, creating the top beam and securing the jetting beams. These were also positioned on each of the lower end panels and on the left-hand porch. The upper prefabricated sections could now be fitted into position resting on the ends of the jetting beams, including both the gable ends, and supporting the upper overhanging gable appearing over the porch.

The Upper Floor

The upper floor could now be tackled, making up the upper wall panels in the same way as the lower walls. However, the timber frame would feature two decorative diamonds made up from four angled braces. This pattern only appears on the front elevation, as the rear elevation was nearly right up to the curtain wall of the castle and would not be seen. This decorative pattern would be repeated on the gable ends, although smaller in scale.

The mullion window frames were not as deep as those on the lower floor, but the glazing style was

The first-floor panels have been assembled together, with stretchers added to give extra strength. The two porches have been started, and the grass has been fixed on to the base using short static grass fibres from the 'Green Scene' range.

Close-up in which the cess pits are clearly visible, along with the finished flagstones and cobbles. The porch has now been extended, with the open window frames fixed into position on both sides. On the top of the wall panels the jetting beams have been fitted, with short spacer timbers in between.

exactly the same. All the upper wall panels were constructed flat, all with the windows added as prefabricated sections. These were all painted in the same way using the same colours again, all before assembly. The finished panels would be brought together and assembled using the posts at all the corners. The corner posts on the upper floor would not be as wide as those on the lower.

The two gable ends would require two slots cutting half-way along the pitch. These were to hold the two purlins, which would run the whole length of the building to support the roof.

CONSTRUCTION OF THE ROOF

With the purlins secured and glued into position, the construction of the roof could now begin. For the sub-base, 1.5mm mounting card was selected; this was measured out, and 8mm added to the front edge, to form the roofline's overlap. The two roof panels will also require 12mm added to the ends, to form the overlap of the roof on both gable ends. The top edge would require about 4mm over and the same under. This would allow for an uneven ridge, a common feature of this type of building.

Both panels were now cut out, allowing for the overlaps and cutting the undulating top edge to

The centre section of the lower floor. The vertical stud timbers have been weathered by dry brushing them with white paint, and the wattle-and-daub panels have been distressed by scratching away some of the paint. The leaded glazing has been fixed into the window frames.

The single-storey porch with the gable and sub-base to the roof added. The door frame has now been detailed with ornate timber beading fitted together with two wooden decorative corbels. The beading was made up from 2mm-wide Evergreen half-round styrene strip. The corbels were laser cut as a special order made to York Model Making.

The main porch with the extended upper gable constructed, with the large deep window fitted. The detailing has been added to the door frame, matching the single-storey porch.

The lower side of the building now connected with the upper side. Note how the upper side is sitting on the jetting beams, also the decorative diamond made up from the timbers, the two boarded doors and the glazed windows.

The sub-base roof, made from mounting card, being fitted to the main porch. The sub-base forming the roof to the main building has already been fitted. This was cut to the full length of the building and sits on two wooden purlins.

Looking down on the sub-base to the main roof: the uneven top edge is clearly visible. This has been purposely cut with a slight dip appearing near to the centre. The roof panels are held with dressmaker's pins until the glue has had time to bond.

form the ridge. The two roofing panels could now be glued into position, securing them to the gable ends and on to the two full-length purlins. The panels were brought together at the ridge and secured with masking tape.

The next task on the roof panels was to fix on the rafter ends, which would be visible. These were cut from 2.5 x 2mm balsa wood, cutting them to length with a 45-degree angle cut at both ends. Once all these were cut they could be glued on to the underside of the overlapping roof panels, spaced out at 12mm intervals.

The next job would be to measure up and cut the roof panels for the two porch extensions. These were again cut from 1.5mm mounting card with overlaps allowed for on the facing and side edges; however, these would only need to overlap by 6mm. The panels on the porches could also be cut square on the top edge to form a level ridge. The same rafters could be added, again glued on to the underside of the porch roof panels.

THE ROOF TILES

With all the roof panels now fixed into position and rafter ends fitted, the entire roof along with the porches requires covering. From archival evidence found on the site we know that the roof was covered with handmade terracotta tiles. By looking at other half-timbered buildings of a similar age a good idea of the tiles used can be obtained. I made the decision that the tiles could be cut from greetings cards, but to create the uneven finish they would need to be cut and placed on individually.

Marking and Cutting Out the Card Tiles

The task now was to start marking and cutting out a few thousand card tiles. The size of each tile finished at 10 x 4mm, which would be to the scale of the model. The tiles were all cut in advance ready for the mammoth task of fitting them to the sub-base roof panels. A start was made by first attaching the tiles to the front edge. To attach the first few rows, a strip of double-sided tape was fixed on to the mount card.

The next task was to cover the whole expanse of roof with individual cut tiles, each tile being cut from 4mm strips of greetings card.

Each individual tile is placed and secured with glue to the sub-base of the roof, with each row of tiles overlapping the previous row, until the roof ridge is reached.

The roof can now be seen with the card tiling completed up to the ridge. The base to the chimney stacks can also be seen, again made up from mounting card and temporarily placed into position.

The first row was fitted to the front and rear of the roof panels with a 2mm overhang included.

Once the first row had been attached, the second row could be started.The tiles would need to overlap the first row by 4mm, to give a visible tile face of 5 x 4mm. On both the first and the second row some tiles were fixed on so they were overhanging slightly more than others – also at the end of the rows, half-width tiles would be needed.This method of fitting the tiles was now continued up the slope of the main roof using double-sided tape initially, and a small amount of impact adhesive to secure the overlap.

The tiling continued until arriving at the ridge, making sure the irregular pattern was followed, with some appearing to have slid down, and quite a few with broken off corners. All this would add to the

The chimney bases have now been removed to allow the whole roof area of tiles to be spray painted. First, though, the rest of the building will need to be masked off before applying a coat of 'Halfords' red oxide primer. This is to give a base colour to match the handmade terracotta tiles originally used to cover the roof.

rustic appearance of this aged roof, giving the desired finish for the model.

Once the ridge had been reached, it would need to be topped out with ridge tiles. These were made up by folding in half small, rectangular pieces of card, each measuring 12 x 8mm. These were folded, making a tent fold ready to use for ridge tiles. Each tile was then glued on with impact adhesive until the whole length of the main roof ridge had been topped.

THE TWO PORCH ROOFS

Once the main roof was completed, the two porch roofs could be addressed. These were tackled in exactly the same way, topped with the same tent-folded ridge tiles.

All the tiled roofs now required painting, which would be done before adding the chimney stacks. The first stage of this was to give all the card tiles an overall coat of red oxide primer. This would be the undercoat, giving a basic background colour of the terracotta tiles. More work would be required to pick out the various shades of this type of roofing material. Finally the tiles would need to be weathered with rain staining and lichen growth.

THE TWO CHIMNEYS

Moving on, the two chimneys could now be built, starting with the two bases. These were measured up and drawn out on mounting card, with the depth measuring 36mm and the width 20mm. The depth was divided in two, with a centre line marked on; next a small piece of card was put up against the gable end and taped on. While this was in position on the gable end, the pitch of the roof was traced on to the piece of card. With the card taken away, the traced pitch was now cut out to use as a template,

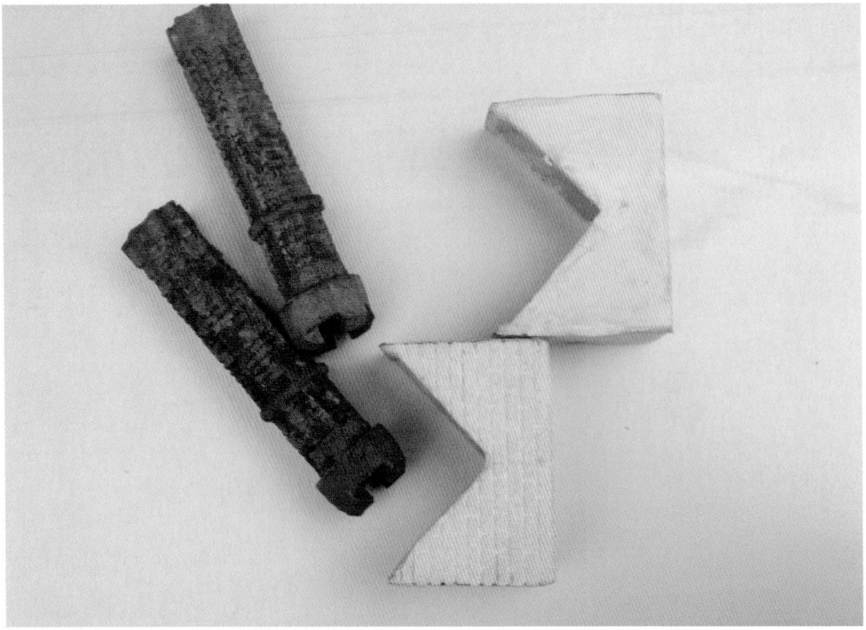

The two chimney bases cut from mount card, and now covered with a skin of Das modelling clay. The brickwork masonry has been scribed out on all the sides, replicating stretcher bonding. The two octagonal chimney stacks have been cast in resin from a wooden carved master. The master was coated with clay and scribed with the string coursing and tops fabricated from styrene.

The two chimney bases, now attached to the roof's ridge. The dip along the ridge is also clearly visible.

and transferred to match up with the centre line on the chimney base before being cut out.

This was repeated, and the bases were constructed. A top was cut out and added, before the base sides were given a skin of Das modelling clay. This was applied only as a thin skin, achieved by adding more water. The bases would need to be scribed out with handmade brick coursing. The tops were left at this stage, as more clay would be added at a later stage to join the stacks to the bases. The bases were left to dry before being painted using brick shades mixed from oil paint (see Appendix: Colour Mixing Guide).

The chimney stacks were thought to have been fairly ornate, as they were a statement of wealth in the Tudor period. The hunting lodge did stand within the grounds of a castle, therefore it is likely that this building, even though only constructed of a timber frame, would have boasted impressive chimney stacks. A little investigation was needed to find some Tudor chimney reference. Most of the ones I found were too elaborate for this building, so I decided to make up a generic version, making it simple but at the same time decorative.

Making up a Master

I also decided that only one master would need to be made up, and the ones to use on the model could be cast from a mould taken off the master. The master started with a piece of wood measuring 12 x 12mm square, cut to 50mm in length. This was then cut away at 45 degrees on all four corners to give an octagonal profile. Each of the eight sides was then fluted. This was achieved using a concaved bladed chisel, carefully cutting away the curved face.

Coating the Stack with Plaster Mix

The whole stack was now coated with a thin plaster mix, using 'Unibond No More Cracks'. This was then scribed with the brick coursing. The handmade bricks used on Tudor chimney stacks were only made to a small size. To finish the chimney's construction a decorative top was required. This would follow the octagonal shape, although at a larger width to the rest of the stack, with the top featuring castellations. This was all fabricated from styrene, with the base marked and cut from 0.75mm sheet. The sheet was cut to the octagonal shape of the stack allowing for 2mm extra added on for the top to overlap the stack.

Fabricating the Sides to the Top

I then started to fabricate the sides to the top, again using 8 x 2mm and 4 x 2mm Evergreen styrene. These were cut at an angle to join up with each other, making up the octagonal shape. All the sides were glued on to the base, with one face made up using the higher piece and the next using the lower piece. To finish the construction the top edge of the higher section was chamfered to a 45-degree angle, before being cemented with superglue to the top of the stack.

Coating the Stack with Varnish

The last task was to coat the stack with a few coats of clear varnish. The reason for adding this was to act as a releasing agent for when the silicon rubber mould was made. Once this was dry, I could send the master off to 'Skytrex 2013 Models' for the mould to be taken, and then resin castings made from the mould. This was the best solution where four identical ornate Tudor stacks were required for this model.

When the stacks had been delivered, the first job was to give the resin castings a coat of red oxide primer. Once this had dried sufficiently, the smaller brickwork of the stack was picked out using the paint mixes described earlier. The stacks could now be joined up with the bases. Each base had two stacks positioned next to each other leaving a gap of only 3mm in between them. These were

The individual tiles were picked out in lighter and darker shades of the terracotta. This was achieved by using a 3mm chisel brush, applying the paint carefully to most of the tiles.

The two ornate cast chimney stacks have now been located with their bases. After securing with superglue, Das was pushed in and around the stacks, before being sculpted to create the flaunching.

secured using superglue again. More Das modelling clay was then applied to fit around each stack, and also on to the top of the brick bases, to replicate the flaunchings.

Locating the Chimneys on the Roof

Both the completed chimneys could now be located on the roof. With the position determined, the tiles could be cut away in the immediate area to create a more substantial join. The base was glued to the roof, and when secure a little extra clay was applied creating the flashings to complete the join. With both the chimneys now connected to the roofline, the only thing left to do was to add more paint to the flashings and to weather the tops and brick stacks.

COMPLETING THE ROOFLINES

The roof of this aged building would not have had any gutters fitted. The rain would have been allowed to run off the roof and on to the ground, either to soak away or, in the case of this building, drain into the stone gutters at ground level. The main additions to the roofline would be the timber barge boards. For the model I decided to use coffee stirrers, as the thickness and width were just right at this scale.

The two chimney stacks now completed; note the dips in the roof ridge.

The gable ends and the porches have now received the facing barge boards. These were simply fabricated using coffee stirrers.

The barge boards fronting the two porches have now been painted to match the rest of the timber framing.

The stirrers were cut to length, and then cut to an angle at both ends. The stirrers were then glued up on to the edge of the card at both gable ends. I also used small pieces of 3 x 3mm balsa wood, placed behind the barge boards to make a more secure join. Besides the two gable ends of the main roof, barge boards would be needed for both the porch roofs. Coffee stirrers were used again in exactly the same way to finish off these two smaller gables. With the barge boards now all fitted, the only thing left to do was the painting and weathering, which would be required to match the timber framing, completing the construction of this historic building.

THE BASEBOARD

Moving to the base of the model, 6mm plywood was selected, and measured and cut out to a total of 12in (305mm) wide by 30in (762mm) long. This would allow for 3in (76mm) extra to the entire footprint. I have already mentioned the stone gutters at ground level, which were situated just away from the walls of the building. Card was first placed around the footprint of the building. A gap of 3mm was left to create the gutter, before card was placed at the front and a small strip at the rear. This would form the sub-base for these small areas of hard standing, where cobbles would be included at the front and both ends of the building.

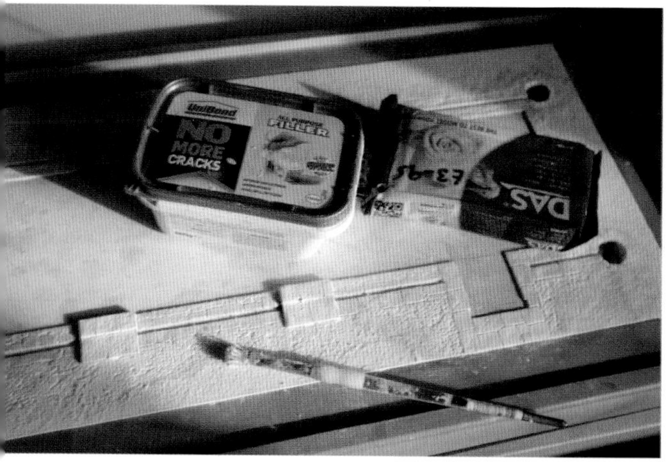

Moving away from the building, here the base is being prepared, with card added first to make up the sub-base for the hard standing. This surrounds the footprint, which has been left so the building fits neatly into it. Das modelling clay has been put down along with 'No More Cracks' ready-mixed plaster. The Das was used to create the flagstones edging the gutters, and the plaster mix to surface the steps outside the two porches.

All the flagstones and irregular cobbles have been scribed out. Also of note are the four cesspits positioned at the end of the gutters. These are supplied on all four corners of the building to take away all the rainwater from the roof, and any other type of waste.

The next stage was to paint the flagstones and cobbles using mixes of artists' oil paints to represent the stone used. I have included a colour-mixing guide at the back of the book. Also at the rear, the ground colour has been applied ready for the grass to be added in this area.

Four holes were cut, each measuring 24mm in diameter, one at each corner of the building and at the end of both the gutters: these would form the drainage/cess pits.

All the sub-base now needed to be coated with a skin of Das. This was applied reasonably thinly to achieve the hard standing materials required. Around the plinth of the building stone flags were scribed into the surface of the clay, while more flagstones were scribed to edge the gutter and the pits. All the other areas were scribed out with irregular stone cobbles. Large flagstones were placed bridging the gutter and up to the doorways – these were coated with 'Unibond No More Cracks' to give the surface a realistic texture.

To finish off, all the hard standing required painting, using colour shades mixed to match these materials.

Another close-up photograph of the front of the building to show the paint finishes, with most of the timbers weathered by dry brushing over lightly with white paint. The door furniture has been added in the form of ring latches.

This view shows the rear of the building, with no windows required: it consists of just the wall panels and vertical timber studs. Also visible are the rear gutter and the grassed area beyond, as no hard standing was required.

The completed model.

Any areas of the baseboard that were not covered with hard standing needed to be grassed. This was simply achieved by first painting the area with an earth colour, before applying static grass. Straw-coloured fibres were added along with green colours to give a more natural effect. Besides the grass, a few weeds and longer dead grass were added, using foam flock and teddy-bear fur. Some flock was also placed along the building's plinth, and some in the cracks between the stone flags.

This now concludes this project to recreate this building as a scale model. For this display model I purposely chose a larger scale; however, using the same materials and techniques it could easily be built in a smaller scale, for example to the popular 4mm (00) scale.

CHAPTER TWO

BUILDING A HISTORIC STRUCTURE: CODNOR CASTLE DOVECOTE

For this project I want to present the modelling of a lost structure: Codnor Castle dovecote. In the last chapter I created a miniature version of a historic building that no longer exists. This prompted me to attempt to model a structure that also no longer exists today, the difference with this project being that the dovecote did remain, although in a very dilapidated state, until 1969. In the first project the original building had been demolished many years previously, with nothing remaining on the site, and no records remaining.

With this structure, a few photographs were taken over the last century. Other visual records also exist, including a contemporary engraving made a few centuries before. Although no actual scale plans of the dovecote exist, the visual recorded material provided a good starting point for producing this model. However, before starting this model, I would like to give a brief history of this intriguing structure, as it is always interesting to know why it existed in the first place before attempting to make a model of it.

A BRIEF HISTORY

Following the Norman Conquest, Codnor, on the eastern side of Derbyshire, was awarded by the Norman lords to William Peveril. The Peveril family continued to live at the manor at Codnor until it was taken in 1155 by King Henry II, when the manor and deer park were granted to the De Ferrers family. Around the year 1206, Henry De Grey of Thurrock married Isolda Bardolf, who had become the co-heiress of the Bardolf estate in Derbyshire after the death of her father Hugh Bardolf 'The Sherriff of Nottingham and Derbyshire' in 1205.

It seems very likely that it was Henry De Grey who was responsible for building the first stone castle on the site at Codnor. The De Greys went on to be one of the most powerful families in England at this time in history, with Lady Jane Grey becoming Queen of England for just nine days. Richard De Grey was a Knight of the Garter as well as Lord Treasurer of England. The last Lord De Grey of Codnor was another Henry.

The next family to inherit Codnor Castle and its estates were the De Zouches, when Sir John Zouche inherited them in 1496. The fortunes of the family at Codnor reached their height as a result of the wealth generated by the several coal and ironstone mines in the park. The noted Elizabethan businesswoman Bess of Hardwick went into service in the household of Sir John and Lady Elizabeth Zouche of Codnor Castle. At this time the castle was not required for any military purpose, therefore most of castle grounds were made into formal landscaped gardens.

However, during this time the castle saw many years of neglect, with most of the buildings falling into disrepair. At this time it is thought that only a small part of the castle was lived in, although the Zouche family had initially extended the castle by adding on the Lower Court. But this was now too much for the family to maintain, and it was left to decay.

In 1634 the castle and its estate at Codnor was purchased by Sir Richard Neile, who was the Archbishop of York and Privy Councillor to the King. The Neile family was responsible for dividing up the estate. In 1682 the resident at Codnor Castle was Sir Paul Neile, although he was likely to have been living in Castle Farm, as by this time most of the castle itself would have been uninhabitable, and a good amount of it demolished.

The prototype photograph shows the preserved dovecote located at Kinwarton in Warwickshire. This is a rare surviving fourteenth-century example of the circular design featuring a conical roof. The subject for our model was of similar construction, although it was built earlier, and unfortunately no longer survives. The dovecote at Kinwarton is now owned by the National Trust, and is well worth a visit.

The castle estate was purchased by Streynsham Master in 1692, by which time the castle was in complete ruins. Later, Streynsham Master leased the many farms of the estate to tenant farmers, with Castle Farm being leased to Christopher Colclough. It was, however, the rich deposits of both coal and ironstone that lay within the Codnor Park estate that would be exploited by the landowner. The estate continued to be passed down through generations of the Master family.

The value of the land was recognized by many local industrialists, including Sir Richard Arkwright who had established his cotton mills at nearby Cromford. At this time Arkwright was pressing for improved and reliable transport links to bring in raw materials. This led to the building of the Cromford Canal, which followed the eastern and northern boundaries of the Deer Park. The canal was surveyed by William Jessop, and a monument to him remains in the park today. The construction of this navigation was under the supervision of local engineer Benjamin Outram, and the canal was completed in 1793. The next chapter will feature a project to build a historic canal cottage standing alongside the Cromford Canal.

Benjamin Outram became well known for his involvement in the origins of the railways. His contribution was the plateway system developed to transport horse-drawn wagons of coal and ironstone from the mines to the nearby canals in the area. There are still many remains of these early railways to be found in the park and local area today if you know where to look; one runs diagonally from the castle ruins. With the early death of Benjamin Outram, the company 'Messrs Outram & Co.' became known as the 'Butterley Company'.

Although Charles Masters had continued to mine on the Codnor Estate, the mines were now leased to the Butterley Company and the Wallis family. The Butterley Company purchased the remaining estate, which gave them complete control of all the mines situated in Codnor Park. The park, castle ruins and the rest of the farms were sold to Mr Bernard Swain in 1968. As owner of Castle Farm he was allowed to demolish the medieval dovecote, as it was considered to be an eyesore and becoming unsafe, and not worth saving.

The dovecote, which sat just outside the limits of the lower court, survived until its demise in the late sixties. Its origin is thought to go right back to the mediaeval period, and dated from when the castle existed in its greatest form. This, and the fact that it is such an interesting structure, made it an ideal candidate for being produced in miniature. It is thought that some of the lower parts of the dovecote are still there today, although they are now buried under a huge mound of demolition material.

The remains of the castle and farm were sold to the National Coal Board in 1978, and eventually to UK Coal. Under the ownership of UK Coal the ruins received some refurbishment under the supervision of English Heritage; this was completed in 2007. In the same year television's 'Time Team' was invited to visit the castle, where they carried out an extensive three-day archaeological investigation of the site. Their findings were very rewarding and have rekindled the history of this forgotten castle. This has resulted in the formation in recent years of 'The Codnor Castle Heritage Trust'.

PLANNING THE MODEL

With the dovecote structure now no longer standing, and no plans or drawings existing, I was only left with photographs to guide me. I managed to find a few on a local history site on the internet, as well as a few in publications. The photographs reproduced on the internet included some taken in colour, which would be valuable when it came to painting and finishing the model. For anyone researching a historic building or structure, it is well worth searching the internet for relevant web sites, picture albums and images.

These images gave me a reasonable idea of the shape of this structure, and I was lucky that one photograph included a farmer standing right alongside the door to the dovecote. This of course meant that by taking the height of the figure into consideration, I could estimate the height of the structure. One way of achieving this is to trace the figure on to tracing paper, and then place the tracing against the full height of the structure: the relative height of the tracing will give a good indication of the height of the structure.

SOURCING THE MATERIALS

Both the shape and the estimated height of the dovecote were not too far removed from those of a card coffee cup manufactured by a well-known coffee franchise. I always like if possible to recycle packaging or other items for making models, and I was delighted that the size of the coffee cup matched a popular scale at which this model could be built.

I therefore produced a scale drawing of the coffee cup, and then added the profile to the outside of

Although the dovecote at Codnor Castle was photographed several times in the past, these photos are now under strict copyright. My solution to this was to create my own illustration based on the photographs taken in the mid-1960s, just before the dovecote was demolished.

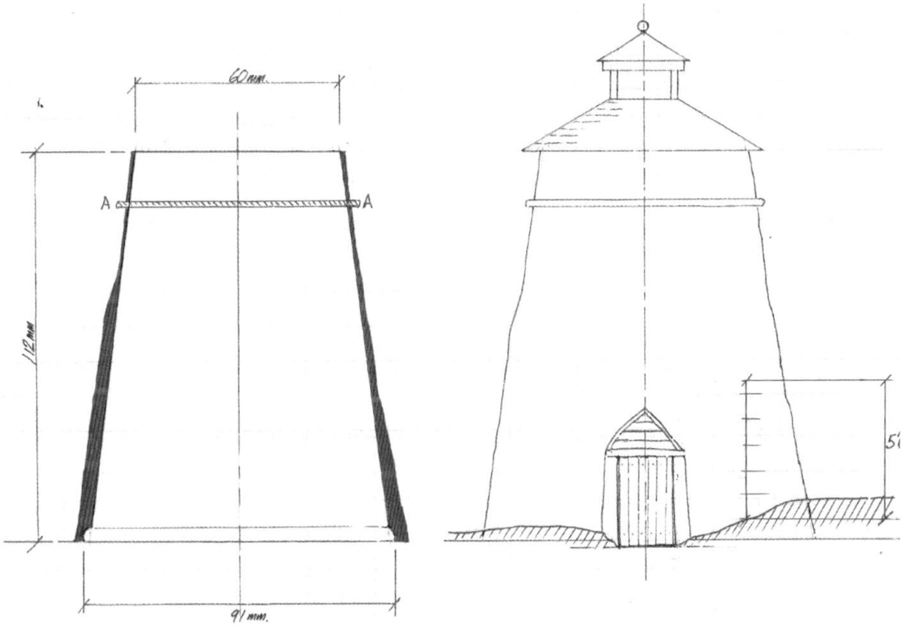

Scale drawing to aid with the construction of this model. On the left is the scale profile of a card coffee cup, showing the thickness of the Das modelling clay that will need to be applied to the cup in certain places to create the actual profile. Also indicated is the raised string course, marked in at A-A. On the right is the profile to the roof, along with the lantern on top. The door and door frame have also been drawn, and alongside I have sketched in the scale of a figure in relation to the scale size of the door and the rest of the structure. The red shaded area indicates the land running up to the dovecote.

A typical card drinks cup that can be used to build a model.

the stone masonry. This was plotted after noting the uneven surface of the dovecote, where one side bulged out more than the other. The drawing would be a good guide as to how much clay would need to be applied to achieve an effective replication of this. The drawing would also determine the angle of the shallow coned roof and the lantern on top.

Other materials were now considered for the construction of this model. A number of coffee stirrers were saved to construct the door, together with matchsticks to use as rafters and as a frame to the lantern. Das modelling clay was to be used for the masonry, and thin card for the roof coverings. This meant that nearly all the materials used for this model were acquired from scrap materials found around the home. This was also true of the scenic setting for the dovecote, where scrap insulation foam and cardboard were used.

CONSTRUCTING THE DOVECOTE

Construction started by cutting the door aperture into the lower front of the coffee cup. It had to be cut to the right shape, with steep angled sides and

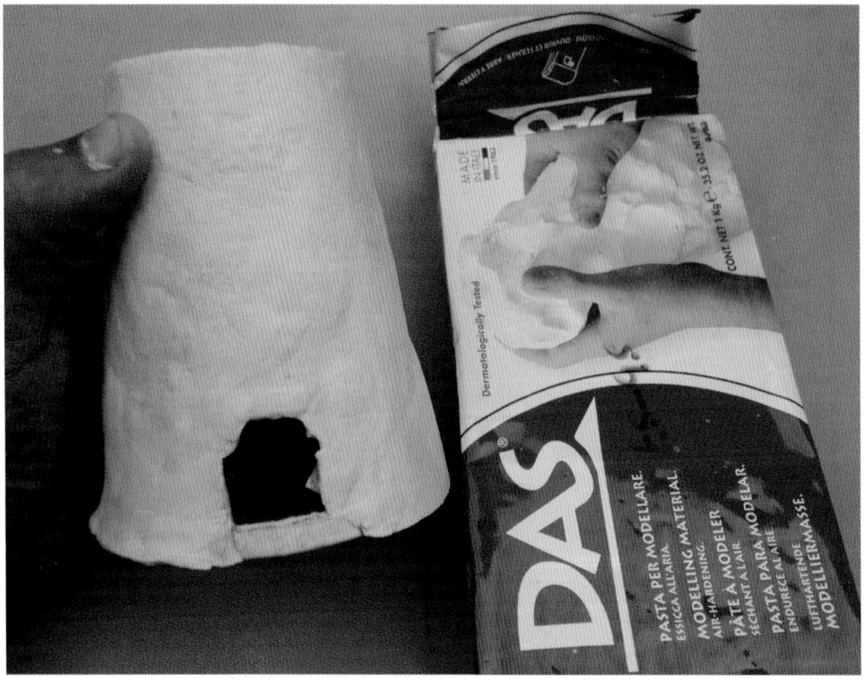

The next stage was to completely cover the card cup with Das modelling clay, trying to follow the profile on the drawing. More clay was added in certain areas, steadily building it up to the desired thickness. As you can see, the doorway has already been cut out; this was done before the Das was added. When applying the damp clay to the thin card cup, it is worth inserting another cup inside to avoid any warping.

a Gothic arched top. The dovecote did not have any windows, which kept things simple, with only the one aperture to cut out. This meant that I could go straight on and apply the Das clay to replicate the structure's rubble stone masonry. The Das had to be applied thickly, and carefully built up, especially on the lower part of the side that bulged out, and this took longer than usual as the profile to the outer wall needed to match the drawing. The clay also took much longer to dry, being applied in layers.

Once the clay had thoroughly dried out and been checked over, I could start scribing the masonry. This needed to replicate the distinctive rubble sandstone of this quirky structure, following the photographic references as closely as possible. I started the scribing with the door lintels and the quoining around the door, with the rest following until the top was reached.

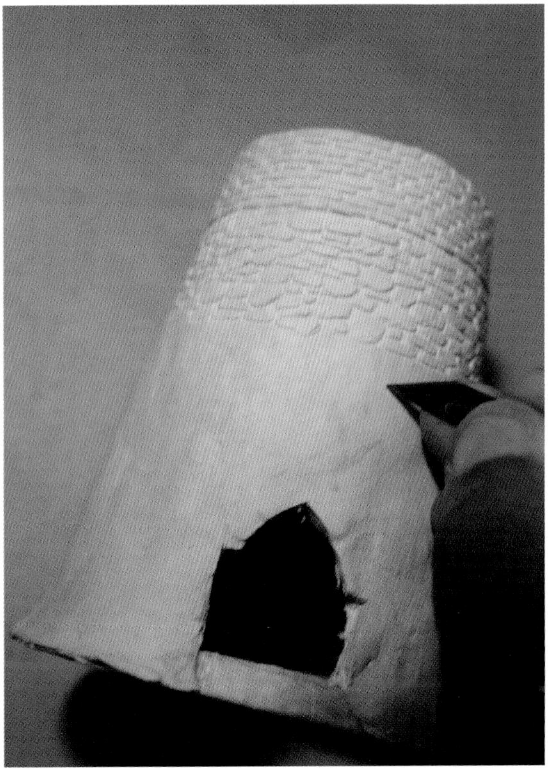

Once the modelling clay has completely air dried, all the rubble stone can be scribed out, working down from the top.

CONSTRUCTING THE RAISED STRING COURSING

The next stage was to construct the raised string coursing; this was positioned near to the top, possibly for the birds to perch on.

This was made using small blocks of balsa wood, each measuring 5 x 3 x 2mm. First, though, a 3mm

The raised string course is being added to the structure. First a 3mm groove is scribed into the clay skin ready to accommodate it. Next, blocks of balsa wood are cut from 3 x 2mm strips, so that each separate block measures around 6mm in length.

All the blocks of balsa wood have been glued into the groove, to complete the string course all the way round.

groove was cut back into the skin of clay. Each block was then glued into the groove until they had gone all the way round. To finish off, the blocks were coated with 'No More Cracks', to give the ledge some surface texture.

PAINTING THE STRUCTURE

I decided that it would be best to paint the structure at this stage, first concentrating on the mortar. This was done using artists' oil paint, mixing Naples yellow, titanium white and a small amount of Payne's grey from the tube, with a good amount of turpentine or white spirit to produce a wash. It was applied all over and allowed to soak into the clay, with capillary action taking the colour into all the scribed-out masonry. This dried in a few minutes, so I could then concentrate on producing the colour of the raised rubble stone.

The colours for this were put out on a palate from tubes, using yellow ochre, burnt umber, Naples yellow, Payne's grey and titanium white. These colours could be mixed together to create the sandstone used for this structure. Extra dry brushing can then be used to blend the shades together, creating a more authentic finish to this type of stonework. It is always best to start with the darker shades first, and then add the lighter shades. More work will be required at a later stage to add any distinctive weathering.

CONSTRUCTING THE DOOR

Before moving on to the roof structure, the door needs to be constructed, though before starting it, I want to look at it in more detail. The clear observation here was its size, which in the photographs appears to be far too small for the scale of the structure. This fact puzzled me to start with, until I did a little research on dovecotes. The reason for a small Hobbit-sized door being installed was for a practical purpose: if a full size door had been fitted, it would let in too much light when it was opened and the birds would fly out. By fitting a half-sized door this problem would be reduced, although the farmer would have to stoop down to enter each time.

Moving back to the model, the door-shaped aperture had already been cut out slightly oversize, waiting for the door to be fitted. The doorframe was

The first painting stage, when the rubble stone masonry of the main structure is painted with a wash of light grey. This is followed by dry brushing over the raised surface of the stonework with shades and tones to match the natural colour of the sandstone. The door and doorframe have also been painted in a dark shade of grey, then a small amount of white is dry brushed over the top to give that aged look.

In this view the dry-brushed stone masonry can be seen clearly. A few prominent stones have been picked out with yellow ochre, again replicating the sandstone used on the prototype.

In this reference photograph, the small doorway to enter Kinwalton dovecote has been featured. Note the interesting shaped door head provided. The dovecote we are modelling at Codnor Castle had a similar door head.

The doorframe, made up from balsa strip, has already been fitted to the model, and awaits the door. The door is being assembled, with the planks cut from coffee stirrers. A strip of double-sided tape has been put down to help with the assembly.

The small planked door is now fitted within the frame. Note that the outside sides to the frame taper slightly.

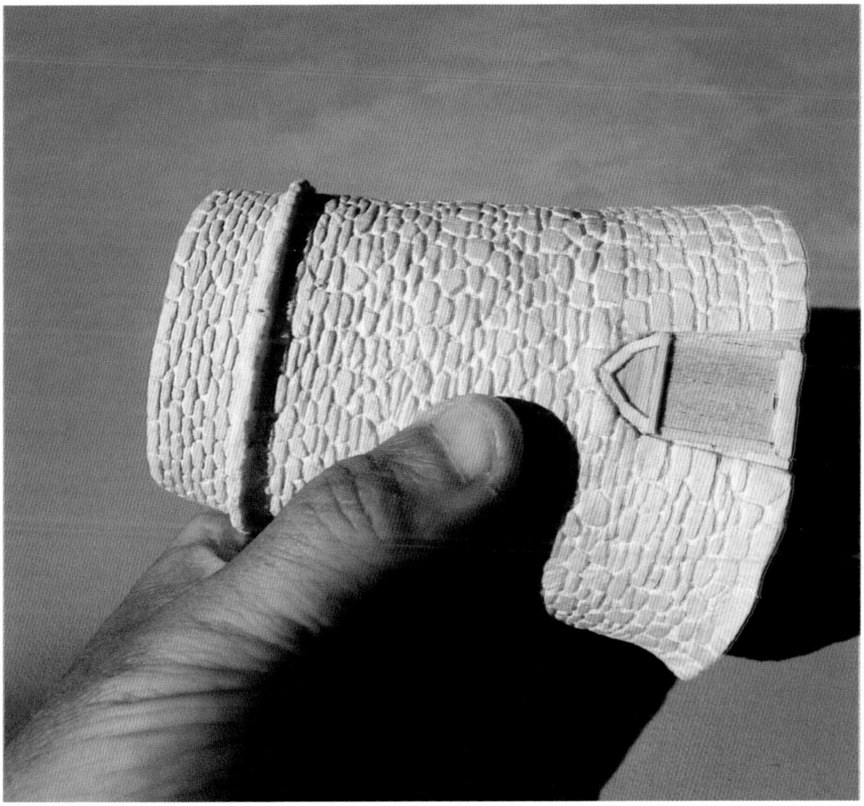

In this view the door head has been fitted, with the gothic arched frame infilled with horizontal planking. The door-head form has been cut from thin card, while coffee stirrers were used to make up the planking.

fitted first: it had a steep angle where it connected to the wall, and a vertical edge to connect to the door. I used coffee stirrers, first cut to length before being cut to shape. These were also used to form the shaped framing of the Gothic arch topping the door. The arch on the prototype was boarded on the inside of the frame, finishing level with the top of the door: I used matchsticks to form this boarding on the model.

Coffee stirrers were used again for the small door, which measured only 3 x 2ft (900 x 600mm) on the prototype; the stirrers were cut to length, and then in half to make the planks. These were assembled side by side and fitted to two stretchers, also cut from the stirrers. I cut these over-length, and cut off the surplus once all the glue had dried. I found it easier to make up the door this way, as you have more control over the assembly. Once the door was complete, then it could be fitted into the doorframe. To finish the construction I also added a wooden doorstep, which helped to make the door assembly more rigid.

CONSTRUCTING THE ROOF

The next task for this model was to construct the shallow coned roof. To start this, a centre post was required, so I needed to find the centre of the cup. With this plotted, a hole was then made to take the post. For the post I used a length of 4 x 4mm wood, which was threaded through the hole and glued. The post needed to stand proud of the cup's top by 25mm and reach to the base of the cup. The reason for the centre post was to support all the roof rafters.

For the rafters I selected a number of matchsticks, leaving them for the time at full length. These could then be laid on the edge or bottom rim of the coffee cup, positioning them about 10mm apart with the ends supported on the top of the centre post. Each rafter would need to overhang the rim by at least 4mm. With the final length marked, the matchsticks could be now cut. The overall effect should look like a cartwheel when looking down on

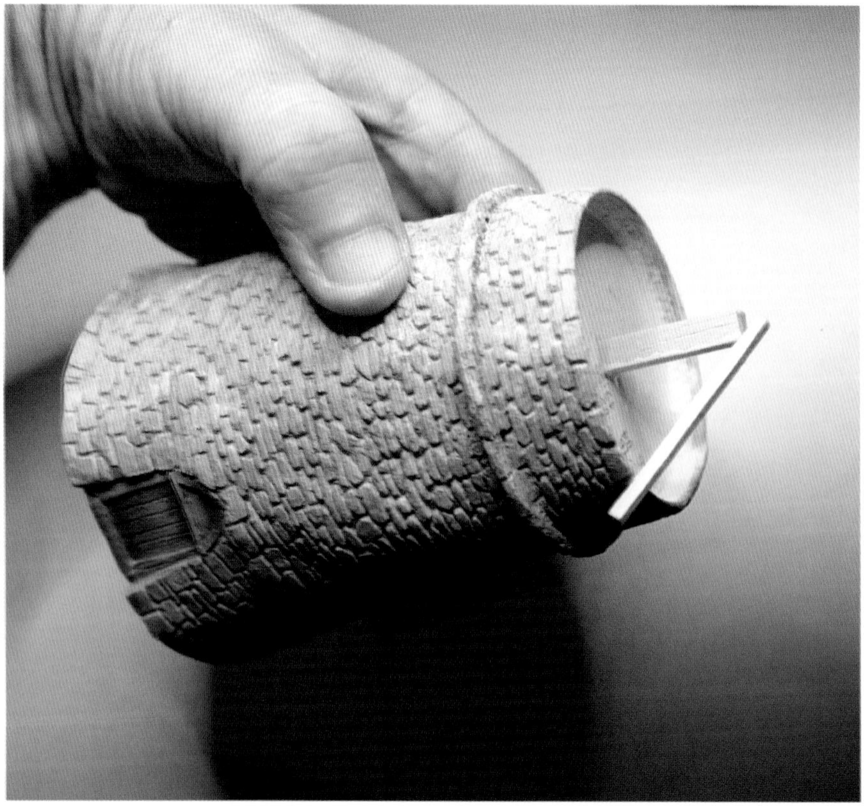

The next stage was to start the construction of the low-profiled conical roof. An upright centre post made from a spent rocket stick was put in place, and the first of the roofing rafters, made from matchsticks, have been added to support the roofing material. These were glued to the central post at one end, with the other end glued to the top edge of the cup, which needed to overhang the edge by 4mm.

the top, with the rafters radiating out from a central hub like the spokes. Once the roof covering was added, only the ends of the rafters would actually be visible on the model.

The next stage was to create a sub-base to the roof ready to fit the tiles. To create this, a measurement was taken of the finished length of the rafters and transferred to a piece of thin card. From this a circle was cut out using a compass cutter, with another cut made from the edge of the circumference to connect with the centre. By pulling the edge of the card along this cut line and threading it under the other edge of the cut, a cone will be formed. Once the angle of the inside of this cone matched the angle of the rafters it could be glued, securing it to the overlap formed. This could now be fixed and glued on to the rafters to complete the sub-base.

The sub-base is now ready to have all the tiles fixed on: these were cut out by hand from thin card again. Each tile was cut to a size measuring 3mm (width) x 5mm (length), although some were cut to a smaller

The rest of the matchsticks have now been glued on to form the supports for the conical roof.

A sub-base was made by cutting out a circle from thin card with a segment cut out. This is then pulled, so that the sides of the cut-out segment are brought together, thus forming a cone. The individual thin card tiles were first cut to size before being glued to the roof sub-base one by one, starting at the edge and working upwards towards the centre. 'No More Cracks' filler was then brushed over, with a little PVA added to give some surface texture. This combination of filler and PVA will also make the roof more ridged.

With the filler now dry, the roof was painted with a base coat of Matt Tank Grey from the Humbrol range of military spray paints. Note that the main structure has been masked off first, by cutting a slightly larger diameter circle out of a piece of scrap packaging card. This was then slipped over the roof, acting as a protective collar while the spray painting commenced.

Some of the tiles are seen here picked out in darker and lighter shades of grey. Note the tiles have not been taken right to the top, but stop short, as the top would be left open for the birds to enter and leave the dovecote under the lantern.

width to fit the shape. Each tile was then fixed on to the sub-base using impact adhesive, starting on the outside edge. This first row of tiles needed to overlap the edge by at least 1mm all the way around. The next row would overlap the previous row by about 1.5mm, and this method would be repeated, rising towards the top. On this model the tiling would not actually reach the top, as the top would be left open to allow the birds to enter and leave.

To complete the roofline a lantern would need to be constructed. However, before building the lantern the roof would need to be painted, using a grey undercoat at this stage. I selected Matt Tank Grey from the Humbrol military range, which comes in a spray can. This meant that a mask had to be made to protect the rest of the painted structure. I used the compass cutter again, to cut a circular aperture out of a piece of scrap card. This needed to be cut

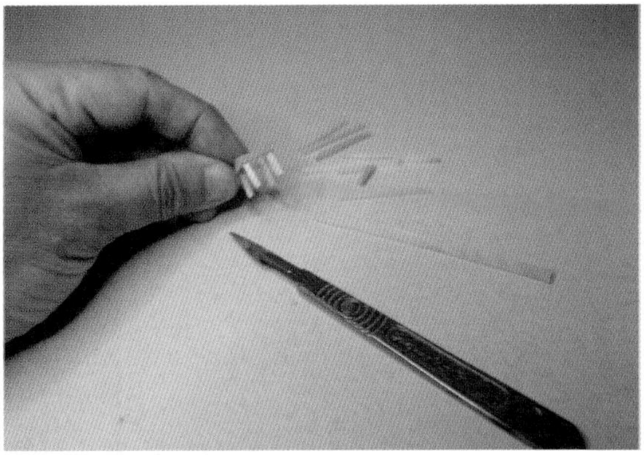

The construction of the lantern has been started by making up the framework. The uprights are made from matchsticks, while the cross-members are again fabricated from cut-down coffee stirrers.

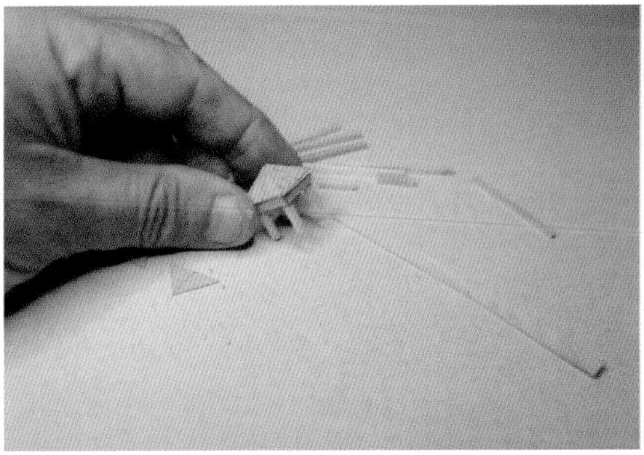

The pyramidal roof topping the lantern. It was constructed using thin packaging card. This started with a base, and then four triangles were marked and cut out. Each side needs to be cut to a 60-degree angle to form the pyramid when all four roof panels are brought together.

The lantern has been finished off and located on top of the conical roof. It has also been painted in a dark grey colour.

slightly oversize, so it would fit over the edge of the roof, creating a protective collar. Once this had been slipped over the roof and held in position, the tiled roof could be spray painted with the grey.

It was now time to build up the roof's lantern: this is provided to protect and give cover for the birds. To construct this for the model, a frame was fabricated using matchsticks: these formed the uprights for the open frame. The stretchers to support the small pyramidal roof were again cut from coffee stirrers. This was made up to size, with the uprights measuring 15mm in length and the stretchers measuring 20mm in length. The frame was then assembled, making the lantern 20mm square and standing 15mm high.

A card base was then fitted to the top, before the roof was made up in a pyramid shape, using card again. This was formed by marking out the card, then cutting four triangles. These need to be measured out first, with the bottom edge (base line) plotted to 16mm long: this needs to be divided in half, with a centre line drawn. A point was plotted on this line at 14mm, and then lines were drawn from both ends of the base line to meet at this point, thus creating a triangle. Once all four triangles had been plotted and cut out, they were then assembled, gluing them first along the base line, and then bringing the angled edges together and gluing at the joins.

The whole construction could then be married up with the roof, and glued into position. The lantern now required painting, first with a dark grey colour, then dry brushed with titanium white to create the silvered, weathered look. At the same time more paint was added to the tiles on the roof, with individual tiles picked out in different shades of grey, with some darker and some lighter than the base colour. This was then blended by using a dry-brushing technique. More weathering was added to the finished roof, with rain-stained streaks and lichens added. A structure such as this built to house doves and pigeons would be susceptible to both staining and lichen growth resulting from the bird droppings.

CREATING THE SETTING FOR THIS STRUCTURE

To set off this structure, a setting needed to be made up. This started with a base cut from 3mm thick card measuring 6 x 6in (152 x 152mm). I wanted to include some raised land, as looking at the photographic reference the structure nestled in the land surrounding it. Looking for materials to create this small amount of land, I settled on using some insulation foam, which would be easy to cut and carve to shape. This was first cut to the basic depth, and then glued to the base. Once this had bonded, more carving was required to create this low land.

The area around the door was left at the level of the baseboard to create a small path leading to it. A small amount of Das modelling clay was put down in this area, and scribed out with a few flagstones immediately in front of the door. The surface of the foam was coated with 'No More Cracks', then painted with a mix of yellow ochre and Payne's grey. This created an earth colour, ready to apply some static grass. I always use a few different colours and different lengths of fibre in the applicator to give a more authentic result. Small amounts of flock were also added around the base of the dovecote, so it blended in with the surrounding land.

The base and surrounding land have been prepared ready to locate the dovecote. The landform has been sculpted from insulation foam, then coated with PVA and plaster. This has then been painted a dark earth colour using a mix of Payne's grey and yellow ochre.

To finish this model I decided to bring in a figure, as not only would this add some human interest, but most importantly it would give a visual reference of scale. Searching for an appropriate figure I eventually found the perfect sample from 'Invertrain', who now hold the 'Border Miniatures' range. The figure chosen was actually labelled as a Whitby fisherman, although I thought that his stance and period dress was suitable for a farmer leaning against the structure. The figure comes as a white metal casting, with very good reproduced detailing.

It first needed coating with 'Halfords' grey primer before any painting started. For this I used the new range specially created for 'Omen Miniatures'. These are pre-mixed to give all the relevant colours needed, which can be used straight out of handy pots. The

The dovecote has been fixed into position and is now complete. The land around the structure has been grassed over using a mix of static fibres and fine graded flock. A few flagstones have been added right outside the doorway. The farmer has also been added, fully painted with super matt acrylic paint. The sculpted white metal figure came from the 'Border Miniatures' range, and was ideal for this purpose. With the prototype long since demolished, at least a record of this historic and interesting structure now exits in model form.

acrylic water-based paint also has very quick-drying properties, and gives an excellent matt finish. This makes the painting stage much easier to carry out, as the figure can be handled between applying each colour, which has got to be an advantage.

With the figure now authentically painted, it could be fixed and glued into position.

This now concludes the building of this unique structure. It was a shame that this historical medieval dovecote had to be demolished. I am sure that had it survived until the present day, it would have been awarded grade two or even grade one listing, with the structure restored to its former glory. At least with the construction of this model it has been preserved in miniature form.

Footnote:A structure such as this dovecote would be an interesting feature for a model railway, as it would fit neatly into a rural farmyard scene.

CHAPTER THREE

MODELLING A HISTORIC INDUSTRIAL BUILDING: AQUEDUCT COTTAGE

For this model-making project I decided to look at another historic building, but this time a cottage that was purpose-built to aid industry. While the first project featured a timber-framed building that no longer exits, this building is still standing, although in a state of ruin.

A BRIEF HISTORY OF THIS BUILDING

In the last chapter the connection of the Cromford Canal with the Codnor Castle estates was explained. Here, the building chosen for this modelling project is directly connected to the Cromford Canal and therefore the industry it served. The canal-side cottage known as either Wigwell or Aqueduct Cottage was in fact built to serve the Leawood arm of the main canal. It was built by industrialist Peter Nightingale in 1802, for the controller of the lock to enter the extension arm.

This shorter canal was built to give access to and serve the industries around the estates of Lea Hurst. These included a number of local stone quarries and lead smelters, but most importantly the John Smedley Mills. This branch canal was originally built right into the mills, but because it was losing water it was shortened in 1819 to terminate at a wharf closer to the junction. The position of the Leawood arm was only a short distance from the wharf connecting the Cromford Canal with the High Peak Railway. This wharf had a transhipment facility, allowing goods to be taken both by canal and on this early railway, effectively giving a through route to Manchester.

The name of the cottage relates to the nearby Wigwell Aqueduct. The cottage stood adjacent to this impressive structure, which carried the Cromford Canal over the River Derwent. It was built as two dwellings for Peter Nightingale's staff, who were employed to work the stop gates to give entrance to his private canal arm.

The canal-side cottage was built from local quarried stone, which included the roof covering. It was possibly the most photographed structure along the full length of the Cromford Canal. It is known that Florence Nightingale visited the cottage when she was living at Lea Hurst in nearby Holloway. Sadly the cottage has not been lived in for over fifty years, with the last occupant living as a recluse. The building never had the convenience of mains facilities – it was lit by oil lamp, and water was collected from local wells or taken directly from the canal and then boiled over the open fire.

From the early 1970s the cottage was left to decay, and nature gradually took hold of this ruin. Trees have recently rooted themselves into the stone masonry, and the roof has completely caved in. However, since I started writing this book, the Derbyshire Wildlife Trust has made a start on cleaning up the ruin, and they hope to restore the cottage to its former glory in the near future. It would provide the perfect location for a visitor centre positioned in the Derwent Valley Mills World Heritage Site.

SITE VISIT AND PLANNING THE MODEL

A start was made by visiting the remains of the cottage on the Cromford Canal. The site was accessible, since restoration work had started. A friend accompanied me to help with taking measurements on site – it is always worth recruiting a few helpers, even if just to hold one end of a tape measure. I

ABOVE: ***The remains of Aqueduct Cottage as it stands today. A considerable amount of undergrowth has already been cleared away from the structure, which is awaiting restoration in the future.***

The building as it looked when it functioned as a lock keeper's cottage.

My Homemade Sighting Pole

My homemade sighting pole is made from a white metal tube obtained from a DIY store – although a broom handle will suffice painted white. This was cut to 4 foot (1,200mm) in length. The length is then divided into lengths equally of 1 foot (300mm), and painted with alternate bands of a bright colour, making a simple surveyor's sighting pole. This can now be used by putting the pole alongside a wall, for example, and taking a photograph of the building or structure including the pole. This is why a bright colour should be used, so it shows up clearly on the photographs taken. The use of the pole will always give a good idea of heights and other measurements, and is well worth considering. (It might be a good idea to obtain permission before proceeding with this method on some buildings or structures.)

also took a shorter measure, a height sighting pole, a notepad and pen, plus my trusty camera.

First all the outside walls were measured and the dimensions noted down on a rough sketch of what was left of the building. This was followed by measuring the walls of any extensions, such as the two sculleries. Next my friend held the measuring pole up against the walls, and I took a number of photographs with the pole in position. The pole gives a good indication of the height of the walls. Another way of roughly calculating the height of a wall is to measure one stone, and then count the courses – though this will only work out if the stones are all of a regular size; luckily this was the case with the cottage. All the height measurements were also noted down, and photographs taken to back up this information.

It is always worth gathering as much information as possible on a site visit, as it will always be valuable when it comes to building the model.

The pitch angle of a roof can be a problem, although I do have a way of roughly calculating this using a folding metal ruler and a protractor. However, this was not possible on this site due to the close proximity of trees and thick undergrowth, as you need plenty of room to stand away from the gable end wall to carry out this procedure successfully.

There were also a few outbuildings around the cottage, including two earth closets. Measurements were also taken of these and photographs taken. Along with the main cottage, a rough sketch was made with the measurements taken added to it.

The next task was to measure up all the window and door reveals, taking them from the inside of the walls. There wasn't much left of the window or door frames, as for the most part they had rotted away. The upper floor windows had to be estimated by counting the stone courses near the sides. The cottage had very prominent stone lintels, sills and vertical stone jambs, while one window had a centre mullion. These were all measured where possible with the shorter tape measure, then sketched on to the rough drawing and their measurements added.

Besides the windows and doors, I decided to measure any other prominent stones on the building, which included some rather large corner quoins. Again, I thought it was worth roughly sketching these, and noting where they appeared on the corners of the building. The two chimneys were next to look at, although again not much remained as they had collapsed over time, and one had been struck by a falling tree. The height and width of this brick-built chimney therefore had to be totally estimated, using old photographs of the cottage for reference.

While on site I made sure that a series of photographs were made including a good number of close-ups, as well as general views. Photographs are a valuable form of reference not only for construction, but also for the painting and weathering of the model at a later stage.

With all the reference material now gathered on site, the next stage was to use all this information to produce a scale drawing.

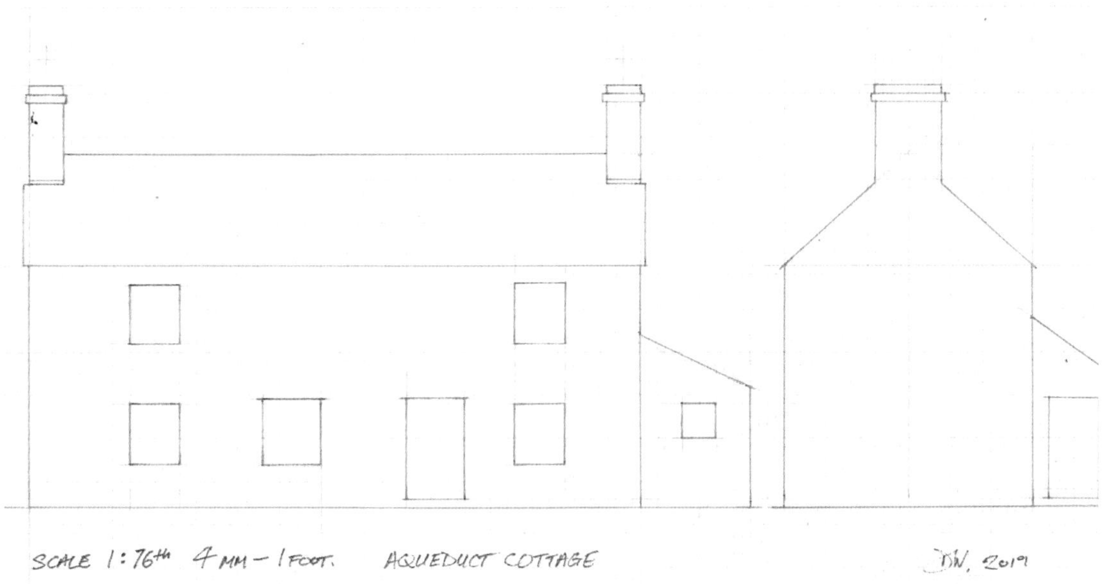

The model started with a scale drawing, made from measurements taken of what remains on site.

MAKING A SCALE DRAWING

The first thing to consider was the scale of this model, which in this case was 1:48th or ¼in to 1 foot. For this display model this would be ideal, although there is no reason why the model could not be scaled down to the more familiar model railway scales. The drawing can be produced on a computer if you have the appropriate software; I don't, so I drew it out on paper with pencil first, then went over it with a fine pen.

A drawing board with parallel motion fitted can help to produce a more accurate drawing. Otherwise a drawing can be made on graph paper using the pre-printed squared grid to help with its accuracy. The drawing needs to include the front, the rear, and both end elevations, as well as a footprint or floor plan if possible. All the details that have been roughly put on to the site sketch will now need to be transferred to the scale drawing, ready to take to the next stage of construction.

BUILDING THE MODEL

I decided that the model of the main cottage should fit into its immediate setting. This requires adding to the depth of the walls on the cottage for it to drop snugly into a foundation. This is of course how a real building would be built, with footings and a foundation provided.

CONSTRUCTING THE MAIN WALLS

3mm foam board was used for constructing the main walls. This material is very light, but at the same time reasonably robust for model making. All the walls were redrawn from the scale drawing, adding another 20mm to the base to allow for them to fit into the foundation. The front and rear elevations should be reduced in length by 3mm on both ends, to allow the roof pitch on the gable end of the end elevations to fit up perfectly when cut out and assembled. The end elevations will also have the chimney stacks added at the apex, and one will need the scullery end wall adding to the rear.

Once all the elevations have been drawn on to the foam board, all the window and door apertures can be transferred from the drawing and marked on to the board.

CUTTING OUT THE WINDOW AND DOOR REVEALS

The next job is to cut out everything that has been marked. It is always best to start with cutting out the window and door reveals, as it makes the process of assembling the walls easier. When cutting out this type of board it is always worth fitting a new, sharp blade to the scalpel or hobby knife; this is especially relevant for cutting out the windows and doors. When cutting the foam board a series of cuts is the best way of achieving a clean, square cut.

Once the main building has been cut out, the extensions and the outbuilding will need to be addressed.

ASSEMBLING THE WALLS

Now all the components are ready for the next stage of assembly. Note that when gluing foam board it is important to be aware that the centre core of polystyrene foam will dissolve if impact adhesive is used. Therefore when joining the wall elevations together always use PVA glue. However, this means that it will take longer for the bond to set, so the join will have to be pinned until it has.

When joining the side walls to the gable ends, the corners will need to be braced. I re-use the triangular off-cuts of foam board cut from the gable ends. It would also be worth adding a stretcher brace to join the front and rear walls together. These are placed with one centred on the top edge, and one centred along the bottom edge.

The two extensions for the sculleries and the earth closet can now be constructed in the same way and from the same materials.

COVERING THE WALLS WITH DAS MODELLING CLAY

The next task was to cover the foam board with a skin of Das modelling clay. This needs to be applied to a reasonable thickness, because on the cottage walls the surface of each stone had the stone mason's surface marks, which would be clearly visible at this larger scale.

The clay was applied into a coat of PVA using the fingers, so as to push the clay on to the foam board's surface. When applying the clay, concentrate on just a small area at a time – doing it this way makes the task a little easier as you will have more control of the clay. Don't forget to keep your fingers wet when applying the clay.

Once the whole of the carcase has been covered with an even skin, leave this to air dry. I would recommend leaving it for at least twenty-four hours before cleaning up and eventually scribing out. Cleaning usually requires sanding the clay on the corners, and using a small file to file away any clay overspill from the window and door reveals.

With this completed, the stonework can be scribed. However, before this can take place, the coursing will need to be plotted and marked on to the surface of the clay.

COURSING AND SCRIBING

Coursing is always required when reproducing regular coursed stone or brickwork, as you will need it to guide you when you get to scribing. The spacing of the courses now needs to be marked on to the walls, working to the desired scale. In this case pencil lines were drawn on to the surface, creating a series of parallel lines; this was repeated on all four walls, including the two extensions.

Scribing can now be started, using a steel rule to scribe along the pencil lines. I used a scalpel with a 10A blade fitted, though you don't have to use a new sharp blade for this, as you will only be using the tip of the blade to scribe with. Other pointed tools can be used for scribing, I just find the scalpel blade gives a good, clean, 'V'-grooved line.

With all the horizontal courses scribed out, the vertical joins can then be put in, creating a stretcher bond. These will need to be measured out, spacing them equally to form each regular cut stone. The vertical joins can be marked with a pencil first if necessary, although shorter lines can be scribed straight in.

The model of the cottage at a fairly advanced stage. The main shell, including the extensions, has been constructed from 3mm foam board. All the window and door apertures have been cut out, ready for the window frames and door to be fitted. The whole shell has been covered with a skin of Das modelling clay. The stonework has also been scribed, including the surrounds to the windows and doors. Painting the cottage masonry has also begun, with colours mixed to match the prototype. The shell of the building has been located into a pre-made foundation prepared on the baseboard. The hard standing around the cottage has been fixed into position, covered with clay and scribed out with flagstones and cobbles. The wall fronting the cottage from the canal has also been made up, with the rubble stone scribed into the skin of facing clay.

The regular coursing will need to be worked on to create the larger corner quoins, lintels, sills, and the upright stone jambs. To make these, more Das clay will need to be added to the areas, going over the pre-scribed coursing and filling in any grooves. Obviously it will need very careful attention to apply the clay in exactly the area required. Any overspill can be carefully removed when the clay has dried. The edges of each stone can now be scribed out to give a good replication of the prototype.

More scribing will follow, this time to replicate the stone-mason marks etched on to each facing stone. This includes the door and window lintels and sills, and any other larger stones used in the cottage's construction. To reproduce these on the model, a scuffing action with the tip of the blade will give the desired finish.

THE TWO CHIMNEY STACKS

Moving back to the construction of the cottage, the two chimney stacks need to be completed, with the sides and the inside wall coming together with the tops and rims. The back of the chimney has already been included on each end elevation. Foam board was used again for the inside wall, and 1.5mm card for the sides. All the components were cut out, with the sides cut to a width of 15mm. The two stacks can now be assembled together with the tops and the 2mm deep rim fitted, all made from the 1.5mm card.

The two chimney stacks will now be covered with Das clay, although the outside wall will already have been skinned. This means that the clay applied to the sides must be carefully blended in with the outside wall. When the clay has completely dried the masonry can be scribed. However, on the proto-

The two chimney stacks built up from mount card. Das modelling clay has been added, and the brick masonry scribed. All the facing stonework has been painted, and the completed window frames have been fitted.

type the two chimney stacks were constructed from brick, and this was replicated on the model by scribing the stretcher bond brickwork. The method for producing this was exactly the same as the regular stonework, but at a reduced size, of course.

PAINTING THE MAIN WALLS

Before adding the windows and doors to the cottage, it is a good idea to paint all the main walls of the building. This makes fitting easier as the reveals will have been pre-painted; otherwise they would have to be painted later, after fitting, and this would cause problems with paint straying on to the frames.

Painting started with filling in the mortar courses with a wash of light grey oil paint, the colour being mixed to 20 per cent paint to 80 per cent turpentine or thinners. The wet mix was then brushed all over the exposed walls, with the immediate effect of the wash soaking into the clay, and capillary action filling all the scribed-out mortar courses.

This was followed with a mix of burnt umber, yellow ochre, Naples yellow and titanium white. These colours were squeezed out from the tube on to the palette and mixed together, then the mixed shades were dry brushed over the raised surface of the stonework. By using this technique the paint applied won't penetrate into pre-painted mortar courses. It is always worth going over with the titanium white and Naples yellow to blend at this stage.

The model can now be left to dry before moving on to fitting windows and doors.

CUTTING OUT AND FITTING THE WINDOWS

The first stage to fitting the windows starts with measuring out all the apertures. These measurements then need transferring to pieces of card – though before this was done I pre-painted the card with a buff spray paint. I selected a stone colour from the Humbrol military range, as it was appropriate for this building. The outside edge of the frame was marked on the card first, then the inside edge, only 1.5mm from the outside markings. The next step is to carefully cut it out, but first, a good quality double-sided tape needs to be attached to the back of the card.

CUTTING OUT THE SASH FRAMES

For cutting out the frames I use a sharp No. 11 blade in the scalpel, which I find to be the best way of getting a clean cut, especially on the corners. The

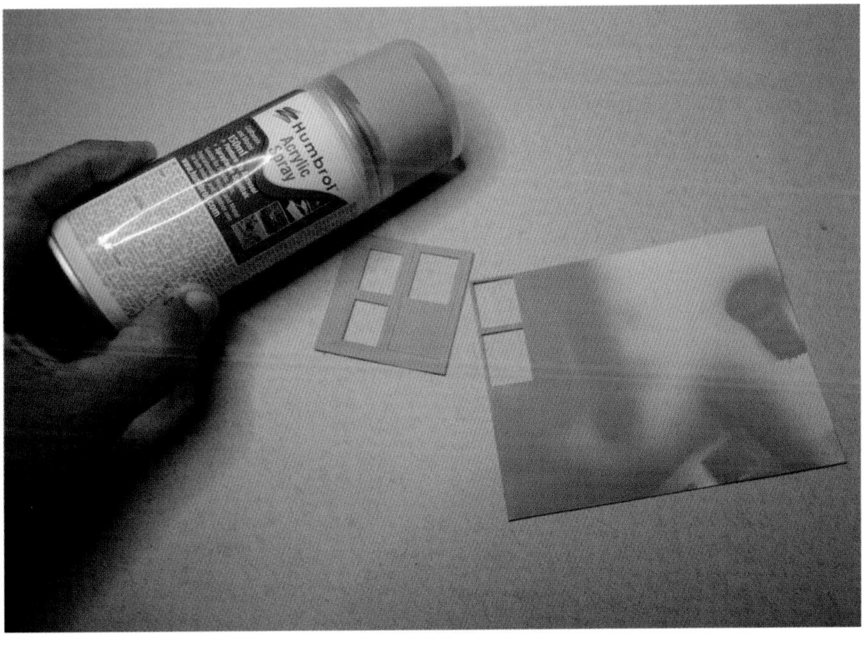

Making up the outer and the inner sash frames for the window frames. They were first measured out, then carefully cut out from old greetings cards. At this stage the frames were pre-painted using a buff colour from the Humbrol military range of spray paints.

The window frames have now been assembled, with the outer frame over the inner sash frames. The inner frame was first fitted with clear celluloid glazing. Double-sided tape was attached to the back of the card before anything was cut out; this made assembly much easier, and kept everything clean. The last task was to add the glazing bars. These were very carefully cut from adhesive-backed labels to 0.5mm wide, then positioned and burnished down on to the face of the celluloid. The fine strips were cut where they met up with the frames, and then coloured with a pen from the 'Winsor & Newton Promarker' range, in a sandstone colour that matched the buff used for the frames.

result will be a frame of thin card, and this will need to be repeated for all the cottage windows. The inner frames are next, and these are marked and cut to the same outer measurements, except this time the inner measurement is 2.5mm from the outer measurement. Follow the same process for cutting out this inner frame to make all the sashes.

CUTTING OUT THE GLAZING MATERIAL

The next stage is to cut out the glazing material: I used some clear celluloid packaging for this. This was cut out allowing 4mm extra on each side of the frame size. The sash frame could now be positioned, and with the backing removed from the tape, it can be fixed on to the clear celluloid. The outer frame can now be carefully placed over the inner sash, making sure everything is lined up. The final result will be a good replication of this type of window.

ADDING THE GLAZING BARS

To finish the sash windows the glazing bars must be added. These were made by cutting very thin strips from gum-backed labels. The labels were first painted using the same spray paint, then thin strips were cut, again using a sharp No. 11 blade in the scalpel. When cutting these fine strips, don't be tempted to cut through in one go, as this will result in the strip curling up like a watch spring. To avoid this happening use a series of light cuts until the strip has been cut away cleanly.

The strips can now be brought in and positioned on the face of the glazing, with one strip dividing the glazed area in half vertically, and another strip dividing the glazing in half horizontally, thus creating four separate panes. The strips were nipped off where they joined the sash, and burnished down carefully. This made up all the four sash widows for this cottage.

THE LARGER REPLACEMENT WINDOW

There remained one other window to fit. This was larger and of a different style, because when the cottage was originally built as two dwellings the aperture was a doorway. This replacement window used two opening casement frames with multiple panes; the two frames were divided with a slender stone mullion. To make up this window for the model, two frames measuring 1.5mm wide were cut out from one piece of card, allowing 3mm for the centre mullion. This time an inner frame was not required, so the single frame was attached to the celluloid.

The glazing bars were made in the same way as for the sash frames, however, both frames were divided vertically into two first, and then three horizontal glazing bars were fixed so as to create eight panes on each casement. The central mullion was then fixed using a strip of mount board cut to 1.5mm wide. This was cut to fit the depth of the reveal and glued into position. A light coating of 'No More Cracks' was painted on to the surface to give it some texture.

FIXING THE WINDOWS INTO THE REVEALS

All the windows were then fixed into the reveals by putting glue on to the overlap left on the side of the celluloid glazing. This was then secured to the inside face of the foam board, completing the task and giving a reasonable replication of all the cottage windows.

MAKING THE DOORS

With all the windows fixed into position, the doors could now be made up. All the doors on this cottage and outbuildings were of the simple vertical boarded type, a good replication of which can be fabricated out of coffee stirrers. The stirrers were first cut

The front vertical planked door made up from coffee stirrers and fixed into the doorway. The frame still needs to be fitted, along with the door furniture. The stone flags making up the roofs have been painted to match the colour tones used for the walls.

to length, and then laid out side by side. Two short lengths of a stirrer were cut and then glued to the rear, with one positioned near to the top and one close to the bottom. The sides were trimmed to make the door fit inside the door frame. All three doors were constructed in the same way, including the one to the privy.

All the doors at this stage were painted a silvery grey colour, which was made up by mixing Payne's grey, Naples yellow and a little titanium white together. More titanium white can be added later, although this will need to dry brushed on.

CONSTRUCTING THE ROOF

The main roof of the cottage was now started, by first measuring up the sub-base. I decided to use 1.5mm mount board, as this needed to be quite substantial. Both panels would have to be cut larger on the two ends and on the front edge by 8mm at this scale. The recess to accommodate the chimney stacks would also be measured and cut out on the top corners. The two sub-bases could now be married up with the end walls. To give extra support for the roof panels, two wooden purlins were fixed half way up the pitch on the gable ends to run the length of the building. With the extra support supplied, the two card panels were glued and secured, ready to take the covering.

CUTTING THE ROOF FLAGSTONES

As already mentioned, this cottage was built using local quarried stone, and this included the roof covering. Large flagstones were cut to cover the lower roof area, and these flags would gradually reduce in size as they reached the roof's ridge. With this in mind,

The roof has been fitted, starting with the sub-base, which is cut from mounting board. The first row of flagstones have been glued along the eves – these larger flags were also cut from mounting board, with the edges chamfered slightly. The chimney stacks have been painted in a mixed brick colour, dry-brushed on leaving the mortar the natural light grey colour of the clay.

In this later view most of the roofing flagstones have been fixed into position, reducing in size and thickness as they advance up the pitch of the roof. Note that the larger window has been changed to represent the earlier style of an eight-paned casement window, with a centre stone mullion.

various thicknesses of card were selected to replicate the flag stones. Thus 1.5mm mount board was used first for the larger flags, then reducing thicknesses of cereal carton board as the flags approached the ridge.

The first larger flags were cut out from strips of mounting board measuring roughly 10mm wide. These were then cut to lengths varying from 15mm to 12mm. Before fixing them on to the sub-base, I carved and chopped the edges away slightly using a sharp blade to create chamfer, although this was not done on all the flags. With this added detailing completed, the first rows could be fixed on, with this row overlapping the front edge slightly. I used impact adhesive to fix the card flags to the card of the sub-base. This was repeated for the first four rows with the usual process of overlapping each row by 3mm, although again this could vary to give the rustic appearance of the prototype.

Moving up the pitch of the roof, the next rows would feature smaller and slightly thinner flags. I found some packaging, where the card used was around 1mm thick. This was ideal to use for the next few rows, with these basically cut out to a slightly smaller size all the way around. The rows following were cut from cereal packaging, which was thinner, but still around 0.5mm thick. This was perfect for the final smaller flags. These were also overlapped in the usual way, with around six rows cut to 8mm wide by 8mm deep. The same process was repeated on the rear sub-base, and when this had been completed the ridge tiles were added.

THE RIDGE TILES

These tiles were fabricated from the same cereal packaging card, cutting them to 15mm in length by 10mm wide. These were then folded in half, forming a tent fold. These were then glued on to the ridge one by one until the entire ridge had been tiled.

TEXTURING AND PAINTING THE ROOF FLAGS AND TILES

The stone flags had an obvious surface texture visible on the prototype, and this was replicated on the model by using a light coating of 'No More Cracks'. This, with PVA added, was brushed over all the flags as well as the ridge tiles.

Once this was dry, I went ahead with the painting, using a mix of oil paint made up from burnt umber, yellow ochre, Naples yellow and titanium white. This was painted all over the roof, making sure that all the flags and ridge tiles were well covered. Extra painting was required to pick out individual flags in lighter and darker shades. This just required adding more burnt umber for the darker shades, or titanium white for the lighter shades, although I did add a little Payne's grey to pick out a few.

THE ROOF TO THE EARTH CLOSET OR PRIVY

With the main roof painted, the next step was to construct the roof to the earth closet or privy. On the prototype this was covered with sheets of corrugated iron. There are commercial moulded styrene or resin sheets available from suppliers that I could have used, however, I found some corrugated packaging that was about the right scale for the model. This came with a card coffee cup, and was intended to be used as a collar, to make it easier to hold the cup when it was filled with hot liquid. This was then cut into individual panels, each measuring 40mm long by 16mm wide to represent each corrugated sheet.

I managed to cover the whole roof with six panels; these were glued on to the thin card sub-base, which again overhung the edge slightly. Each panel would also have to overhang, with the front sheets overhanging the rear sheets. The overhang here was slightly staggered to give a more authentic appearance.

The panels were now painted using mainly spray paints, with most from the Humbrol range. I started by spraying over all the panels with 'Matt Tank Grey'; this was followed by going over with a very light coating of red oxide, which was a primer available from 'Halfords'. Finally I gave another light coat of metallic 'Aluminium' spray paint, again from the Humbrol range. To finish this roofing I dry brushed some cadmium orange on the sides and ends of the sheets to represent rusting.

Moving away from the main cottage, the earth closet or privy has been constructed from foam board and mounting board.

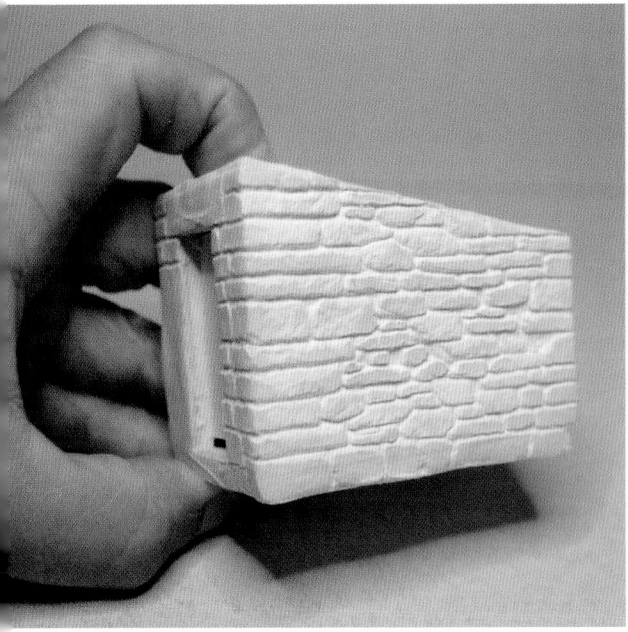

The shell of the privy has been covered with Das, and all the rubble stone masonry has been scribed, starting at the front corner, with the quoins scribed first.

The corrugated sheets cut out ready to fix on to the privy roof. They have been cut from a cardboard collar designed to help hold a card cup full of a hot liquid. This made a good scale replication of the actual metal sheets used to roof this outbuilding.

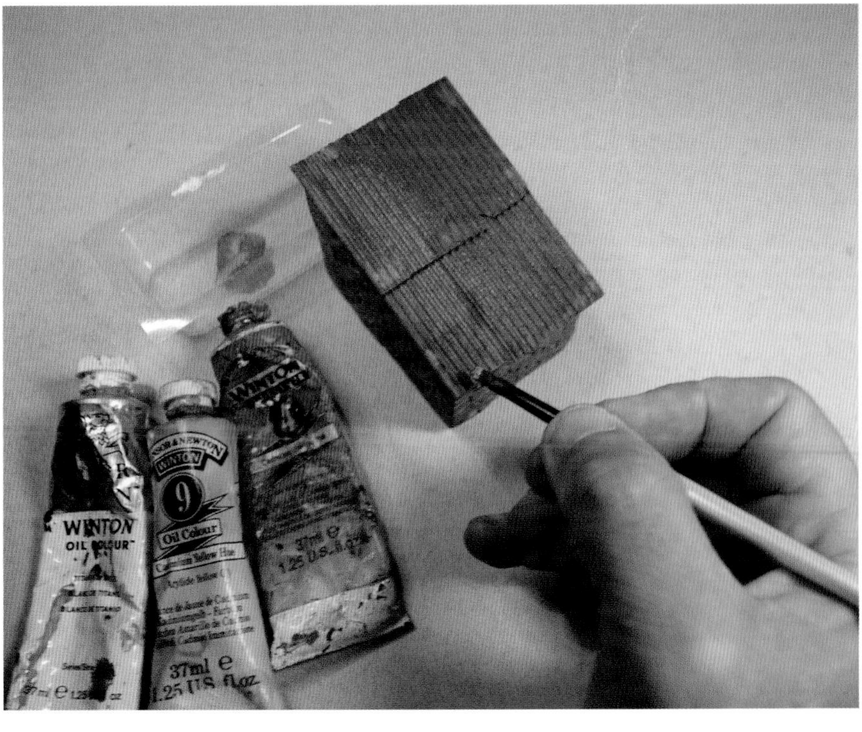

The corrugated sheets fixed to the roof in position. They were painted first using red oxide primer, then with metallic aluminium from the Humbrol spray paint range. This was applied in a light coating so some of the red primer showed through. The next stage was to use a mix of cadmium orange and cadmium yellow with just a little titanium white added. This was brushed on to the edges of the sheets to replicate rusting.

COMPLETING THE CHIMNEY STACKS

Moving back to the main cottage, the chimney stacks can now be completed, starting with painting the brick masonry. This was applied using mixes of oil paint, with cadmium reds and oranges used together with raw umber, Naples yellow, titanium white and Payne's grey. The technique used here was to pick out the individual bricks in lighter and darker shades to match the variations seen in this type of brickwork. Payne's grey was added to create the soot staining found near the top of the stack.

The actual top of the stack could now be addressed, with the pots fitted and the flaunchings added that fixed the pots in place. The pots came from S&D Models, who supply a good range of authentic chimney pots for this scale. The selected white metal castings were positioned, and a hole drilled to accommodate the locating peg on the base of the casting. The pots were then glued on using superglue. Once all the pots had been located and secured, Das modelling clay was pushed around the base of the pots using a dentist's probe or coffee stirrer. This was manicured until a smooth result was achieved, rising gradually from the edge up to the pots.

Once the clay had dried, both the flaunchings and the pots were painted, again using oil paint. I used yellow ochre with a little Naples yellow added for the pots. I also added a little Payne's grey near to, and on the tops, to represent the soot staining. The flaunchings were painted using Naples yellow, titanium white and a small amount of Payne's grey.

This now completed the two chimney stacks required for the model.

ROOFLINE DETAILS

The cottage did feature roofline details, with guttering and downpipes fitted. For the gutters I used a moulded 3mm 'U'-shaped styrene strip available from 'Plastruct'. This was painted with the same buff-coloured spray paint that was used for the window frames. The strip was cut to length before the top of the rear edge was superglued to the underside edge of the facing sub-base roof panel.

The down pipes were fabricated from 2.5mm styrene tube. Styrene can be bent to form swan necks by immersing it in boiling water for a while, which will make it sufficiently pliable to make any desired bends. However, it goes without saying, be very careful when using boiling water. Any collars on the joins can be made by first cutting 2mm strips of tape, and then wrapping them round the tube. Once happy with the thickness the tape can be cut, before burnishing this down to create a tight fit. The pipe can then be spray painted in the same buff colour as the guttering, and fixed to the underside of the guttering and to the wall.

Small 2mm-wide strips can also be added to form the joins along the guttering, as well as filling in over the ends of the gutters. Any extras added will need to be touched up with buff paint to match.

FITTING THE COTTAGE INTO THE CANAL-SIDE SETTING

This model stands individually on its own base; however, there is no reason why it could not be fitted into a selected baseboard area on a model railway. On the surface of the base I started to construct a box out of 3mm foam board from strips cut to 20mm wide. The box was made to accommodate the foundation of the cottage, so the inside measurements of the box needed to be the same as the outside walls of the cottage. Don't forget, though, that an extra 1mm would be needed on the box's length and width to allow the cottage to fit snugly into its foundation.

CONSTRUCTING THE FRONT WALL

The next job was to fit up the front wall facing the canal. This was higher than the land behind it, and was made on the model from a strip of 10mm thick balsa wood measuring 30mm in depth and cut to nearly the full length of the baseboard edges. Before this was fitted into position it was given a skin of Das modelling clay applied to a reasonable thickness. This was then scribed deeply with random stones to match the prototype.

Once dry, the wall was brought into position running at a slight angle to the front of the cottage. Part of this wall would accommodate a small flight of steps leading to the canal. This was allowed for by making the wall lower on the right-hand side. The wall was glued to the base with the steps made from pieces of 6mm foam board, starting with the lower step first, cut to measure 15 x 30mm. The second step followed, fitted on top of the first at roughly half the width. Both treads to the steps were coated with 'No More Cracks' plaster mix, and Das was then added to the sides. To finish the construction of the wall the coping was added, using a 12mm-wide strip of 3mm canvas board. This was coated with a thin skin of Das, before all the joins were scribed, separating the individual coping stones.

BUILDING UP THE LAND BEHIND

With the construction of the retaining wall now complete, the land behind needed building up. I again used 20mm strips of 3mm card, starting with linking the wall to the foundation box of the cottage, with the strips placed and glued in, leaving a 50mm space between them. To this I added cross or stretcher pieces of the same card strips, to end up with a raised, grid-like construction. This was mainly to support the hard standing located immediately in front of the cottage. A simple card base was fitted on top of the raised grid, and a skin of Das modelling clay was applied. When the clay had dried, the hard standing was scribed out, consisting of large irregular cobbles, together with a few flagstones near to the cottage.

The card support was extended on the right-hand side to accommodate the stone-built privy, and wrapped around this end of the building to include the lean-to scullery. Once this had been fixed on, a card topping was fitted, before the area was coated with clay and scribed to match in with the rest. This area was also built into the sloping ground of Lea Wood; therefore some retaining walls were needed to hold back the earth. These were constructed from 6mm foam board and cut to a depth of 30mm. All the retaining walls around the cottage were faced with Das modelling clay, before being scribed with the same rubble stone as the canal-side wall.

PAINTING THE COBBLES AND THE WALLS

To finish the walls, coping stones were added using 3mm card, and coated in the same way as before. The last task was to paint the hard-standing cobbles and all the retaining walls, the colour of which more or less matched the colours and shades used for the masonry of the main cottage. However, the front retaining wall facing the canal needed to be painted in a slightly darker shade to represent the effects of weathering. In particular this was more obvious at the bottom, where it was close to the waterline of the canal.

THE CANAL

A small section of the canal was to be represented at the front of the model diorama, on the section of baseboard left immediately below the front retaining wall. I had used an elliptical-shaped baseboard for this model, so the front was curved where the canal was to feature, so the widest part was 4in (100mm) away from the front retaining wall. The canal's surface was prepared by painting straight on to the baseboard with a mix made up of artist's oil paint; the

The surface to the canal is painted on using three coats of gloss picture varnish.

colour was mixed from the tube using 60 per cent of Payne's grey with 40 per cent yellow ochre. This gave a muddy, dark, olive-green colour, to represent the depth of the canal.

Creating the Surface of the Water

Once the reasonably thick coat of paint had dried, I used three coats of Windsor & Newton gloss picture varnish to create the surface of the water. This type of varnish dries fairly quickly between coats and gives a good reflective surface. On the last coat applied I used a technique where the varnish is applied in small random strokes, and as long as all the strokes are applied in the same direction, a good effect of the water rippling on the surface can be achieved.

Adding Some Natural Growth

The next task on this model was to add some natural growth, especially along the water's edge of the canal. A good idea of the type of plants required was obtained by looking at both photographs taken recently on site, along with a selection of archive images. There was evidence of reeds immediately on the water line, but also a number of plants growing out of and over the retaining walls. These included ivy, which was also a prominent feature on the cottage walls in some of the photographs.

Starting with the marginal plants on the canal, I selected some reeds from one of the scenic suppliers, although others were made up from the bristles of an old household paintbrush. The brush had seen better days for its intended purpose, but it was perfect for replicating reeds. I had used them previously to edge the mill pond on the 'Hay Wain' diorama featured in my last book. All the reeds were cut into clumps before carefully placing them in position and then gluing them.

Other marginal plants were included, made up from shredded foam and various flocks. The ivy was made up using a mix of that supplied by Mini Natur, and the green dyed bracts available from 'Green Scene'. These were attached to the side of the cottage walls using a spray adhesive. The plants clinging to the retaining walls were also made from various foam flocks, attaching them into the gaps and overhanging the coping stones.

COMPLETING THE MODEL

To bring this project to a close, I decided to dress out the model to include a couple of figures. In one of the archive pictures the lady of the cottage was seen clearly standing outside the door. In another photograph the same woman was sitting on the steps with a bucket, ready to take water from the canal. It is always

The marginal plants being fixed along the edge, up against the facing wall. Various scenic materials were used here, along with the bristles of an old paintbrush. The ripples on the surface of the canal were produced by a stippling action used in the last coat of varnish.

The model of Aqueduct Cottage nearing completion. The chimney pots still need to be fixed, along with ivy growth on the walls of the cottage. The results of the varnishing can be seen here, with authentic reflections clearly visible.

worth trying to replicate little cameo scenes such as this, as they will add interest and bring a model to life. I found a figure in the 'Border Miniatures' range (now available from 'Invertrain'). She was labelled as a 'fish wife', but the dress of the figure did match the dress in the period photograph. I used the new range of paints from 'Omen Miniatures', which are ideal for painting figures, with their quick-drying properties and super matt finish.

There is also a nice sculpted seated gypsy figure, in a period range available from S&D Models. This would be ideal to replicate the woman sitting on the steps. Other dressings can be found in this range, which would be worth including for this model. Domestic accessories such as buckets and washing baskets, for instance, would all add to the scene. Small accessories were added to the yard, with a series of rope-topped edging tiles and a boot scraper placed next to the front door.

I also considered adding a domestic cat to this model, either standing alongside the woman at the door or by the woman seated on the steps, as this would add a nice finishing touch. I also thought of including a group of ducks or a couple of swans on the canal. When adding dressings such as this, it is always worth looking at photographs to achieve authentic groupings. It can be tempting to overdo the dressings and the results will only look false, but if the finishing touches are addressed correctly, they can create a model you can be proud of.

CHAPTER FOUR

CREATING AN IMAGINARY BUILDING: 'THE GAMEKEEPER'S HOVEL'

This chapter presents a project in which a model of an imaginary building is made. The one I have chosen will be familiar to some readers, as it is based on a structure that features in a well-known series of films. For copyright reasons, in this book I will refer to it as 'the gamekeeper's hovel', although some readers may think of it by a different name!

SEARCHING FOR REFERENCE

When trying to build an imaginary building or structure it is worth trying to find a prototype on which to base your model. For this building I found a stone-built hovel that was suitable, although I changed the shape and roofline in order to produce

The finished model of the gamekeeper's hovel.

Although the shape of this hovel photographed at Blists Hill is not the same as the model, I have used it for reference as it is constructed from rough rubble stone, which would be similar to that used for this imaginary building. The tiles were also used, as they would be ideal for the project building. In fact the building has so much rustic charm, all of which could be used for the gamekeeper's hovel.

what I wanted. The prototype can be found at 'Blists Hill Victorian Village'. The museum forms part of the Industrial World Heritage site at Colbrook Dale, which is lauded as being the birthplace of the Industrial Revolution.

The prototype building has a rectangular footprint with four walls consisting of large, irregular stones. It has a tall, hipped roof covered with handmade tiles. For this project, however, I changed the footprint and walls to a quirky octagonal format, and therefore also the roofline, which had a central spire. The building materials used for the prototype were ideal for this project, and were therefore used for reference.

PLANNING THE MODEL

CREATING A SCALE DRAWING

The next stage was to plan the model by first creating a scale drawing. With this being an imaginary building, there were of course no actual measurements to work from. The photographs taken of the prototype were only to be used as reference for the stone masonry and the roof covering. The measurements from which to produce the scale drawing would have to be estimated. For this model I decided to work to a scale of 1:48th (¼in to 1ft), with the drawing drawn

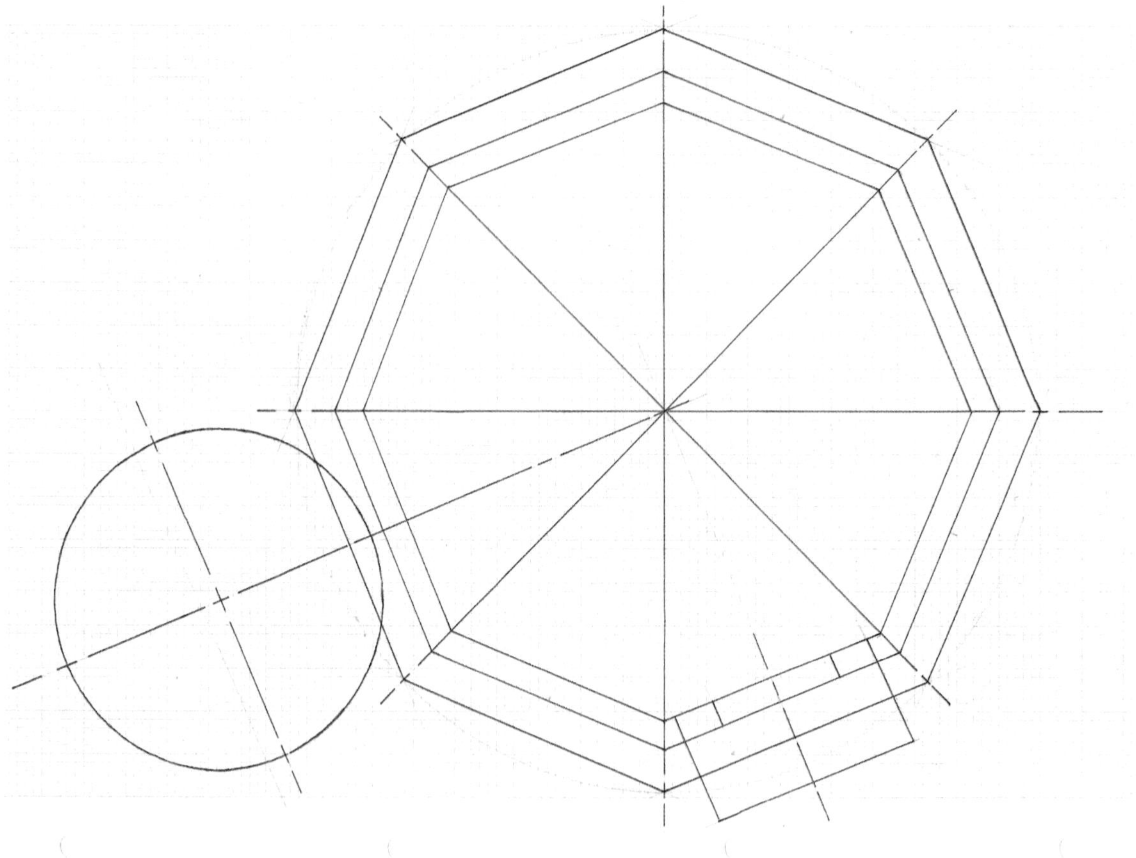

Besides producing the sketch, a scale plan was drawn up to help with the construction of this model.

to this scale. The gamekeeper's hovel also featured a round structure used as a store. In the series of seven films this structure only appeared in the first two; from there on, the hovel included a smaller, quirky extension that followed the same style as the main structure.

MAKING A START ON THE MODEL

MAKING UP THE WALL SECTIONS

The floor plan was used as a template first, then the floor was marked up and cut out from 3mm card. This would be the starting point for the model. The next step was to build up the wall sections, and this would be a challenge due to their angled shape; as the facing wall was angled back slightly, angles were also required at the joins. To make up the wall sections I used foam board for the facing wall, and mount card for the inside of the facing wall, together with the footing made for each section of wall.

The next task was to cut the 6mm-thick foam board of the outer facing wall to size. If the section included a window, then the aperture was also cut out using a sharp blade to give a clean cut. When cutting window apertures don't be tempted to cut through in one go: use a series of cuts, and make sure you cut into the corner. I use a sharp No. 11 slender blade in the scalpel, as this makes sure the corners are cut cleanly. Once cut, the back inside wall is cut from the mount board again, and a window aperture cut out in the same way if the section requires one.

The side walls were all marked out first on to a strip of Corri-Cor board.

The marked strips with one cut out are seen here; underneath are some of the wall panels, which have had Das modelling clay added.

This was then glued to a strip of mount card measuring 10mm wide, leaving the length over at both ends. The centre of the strip was plotted and marked, along with the centre of the rear walling section, and these were lined up before gluing the rear wall to the back of the strip in an upright position. Next the facing wall of foam board was glued to the front of the strip, then leaned back at the steep angle to locate with the top of the vertical inside wall, and glued again.

This was repeated on all the other sides – the four walls with window apertures, the wall with the door aperture, and the remaining three walls that were left blank. The next job was to fill in the gaps between the outside and inside walls: I used thin card for this, the sides being cut to depth, leaving the front and rear left oversized. Once the sides were glued and secure, any card left over was cut flush. The base or sill was cut to fit the aperture first, offered up and glued into place. Any card remaining was again trimmed off flush

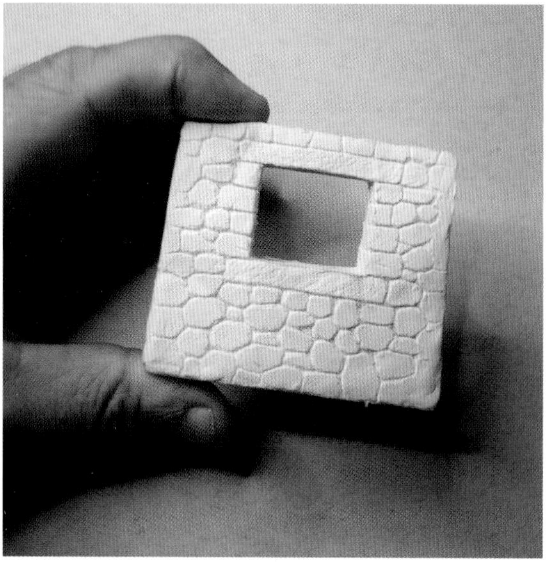

One of the panels has been completely scribed out with the rough rubble stone, together with the lintel and sill to the window.

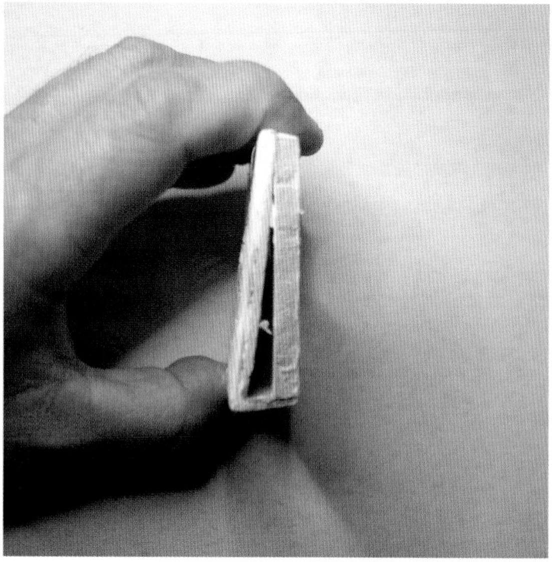

The profile to the wall panels, which clearly shows that the inside wall remains vertical while the facing wall sits at a steep angle to it. The two walls are connected to a base at the bottom, while at the top they meet with each other.

The various stages of construction to the wall panels.

with the facing wall, and with the face of the mounting card at the rear. The door side gaps were filled in using the same method.

The eight made-up wall panels could now be covered with a thick skin of Das modelling clay. The clay was applied into a coating of PVA in the usual way, leaving it to air-dry for twenty-four hours. The next task was to scribe out the rough irregular stone, using the photographic reference taken of the hovel at 'Blists Hill Victorian Village'. The scribing was made reasonably deep to replicate this type of stone, and some surface texture was scratched on to each stone to represent the obvious visible grain. The scribing also included the lintels and sills for the windows, and the stone lintel over the doorway.

MAKING UP THE WINDOWS

The window frames at this scale would be quite simple, with the outer frame divided into two sections, with one side opening for ventilation when required. Just as with the hunting lodge model, I decided to use matchsticks, as they would give a good representation of this style of window. The matchsticks were first cut to the length of each aperture, then the uprights were cut so they fitted neatly up to the recessed walls.

Once all the outside frames had been fitted, then the centre upright could be cut and fitted to divide the window frames into two sections of glazing.

The wooden frames were painted using a thinned-down oil paint mix of Payne's grey and a little Naples

The windows under construction, starting with the outer frames all made from matchsticks. The inner casement frames can be seen cut out from card, which has been pre-spray painted in a dark grey colour.

The window has been fitted, including the diamond leaded glazing, which has been fitted up to the back of the inner frame.

yellow and titanium white. Once the frames had dried off, the glazing could be addressed. I used the same pre-printed, diamond pattern, leaded sheets supplied by 'Freestone Models'. The celluloid sheets were cut to the size of the inner edge of the frames and glued to the inner side of the frame. I did not attempt to make the opening frame as a separate item, as it wasn't really necessary.

THE PORCH AND FRONT DOOR

The section with the front door also required some extra constructional work: to build up two stone pillars to support the porch roof. These were cut from 2mm card, making up two sides and a front. Small pieces of balsa wood were used on the join to make the construction more rigid. Once the two pillars were made up, they were fitted on each side of the door aperture. The two pillars now required Das adding to create the stone facing. This was applied more thinly here to replicate the more dressed

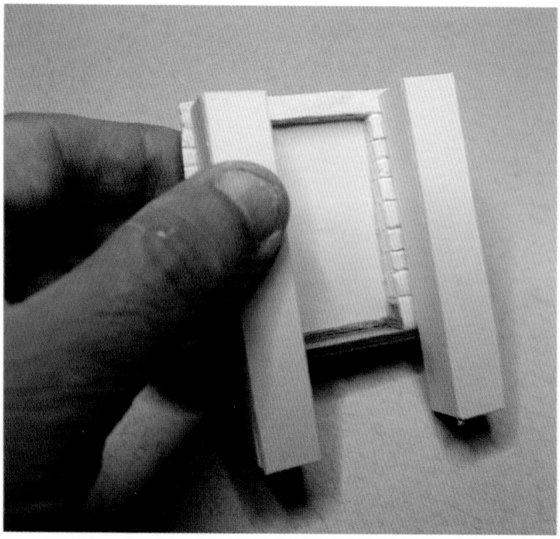

The wall panel with the door to the hovel also required two pillars. These were positioned on each side of the doorway to support the porch roof. The pillars are seen here, constructed from mounting board.

stone used for the pillars. The scribing would follow; however, here a more regular pattern was required to replicate this type of stone.

The front door was assembled next, again using coffee stirrers cut to the correct width and length. These were placed side by side to give the desired effect of the planked door, and were secured with extra lengths of the coffee stirrers to make the stretchers on the inside. The door was then brought in to be fitted up, with extra thin lengths of the stirrers cut to make up the door frame. These were all glued in to complete the door; all that remained was the painting, for which the same paint mix was used as the window frames. It was easier to fit all the windows and the door complete before the walling sections were fitted up to each other.

PAINTING AND ASSEMBLING THE MASONRY

Before fitting the wall sections together I decided to go one stage further and paint the masonry. This was done by adding the mortar, comprising a wash of oil paint, and then by dry brushing the stone shades over the face of the scribed out clay. More paint-

Both the floor and the roof base were marked and cut out from Corri-Cor board, following the plan drawing.

All the side wall panels have now been assembled together, and fixed to the octagonal floor panel. All the joins have been filled with extra Das, and scribed to connect them with the next wall panel.

The scribing is clearly visible, creating a neat join.

ing would have to be done once the sides had been joined together; however, I thought it was worth trying to paint as much as possible at this stage of construction.

Once all the painting was dry, I could assemble all the wall sections together. The first stage was to mark and cut out the floor from 2mm card – I had already prepared a scale drawing of the floor footprint to use for this. The made up side panels could now be fitted in position and glued together. Any gaps on the eight corners could be filled with a little more of the Das clay.

Once this had dried, the stone masonry could be continued by scribing around the corners.

ADDING INTERIOR DETAILING

With this construction completed, some interior detailing was added, including the chimney breast, fireplace and a large high-backed settle. It was debatable if these would be seen on the completed model unless the interior was to be lit, but I thought some interior detail would be worth the effort at this scale for anyone peering in through the windows. All these features were constructed from mount card and painted in appropriate colours.

CONSTRUCTING THE ROOF

The ceiling or base to the roof was now required; again, this was cut from 3mm card and was a repeat of the flooring panel. Once cut out, this was attached and glued to the top of the wall sections, with an overlap of 10mm on all eight sides. The side with the chimney stack would need a recess cutting out to accommodate it.

THE ROOF TRUSSES

The construction of the roof could now begin, starting with the roof trusses. These would feature two angled pitches to support the roof, with the main pyramidal roof at the steepest angle. The roofline at the lower level was at a shallower angle. The first

The octagonal roof base fitted on the walls, with the first few roof supports glued into position.

stage was to plot the two pitches, beginning with finding the centre of the building. This was achieved by drawing a line connecting all the eight corners of the roof base. Where they all crossed with each other would determine the centre.

I used 2mm card for the roof profile trusses, and marked out the width from the edge to the centre first. The next task was to determine the height of the highest point, this being at the centre. A vertical line was drawn up from the centre and the height marked; then a line was marked in at 45 degrees from this point to the horizontal base line. Next a line was drawn in from the outside edge at 30 degrees to meet up with the 45-degree line. This now created the profile of the roof, with the shallow and steep pitches plotted.

CUTTING OUT THE EIGHT PROFILES

The next stage was to cut out all eight profiles ready to support the two-pitched, pyramidal-shaped roof. These were then glued on following the lines drawn on the roof base. One thing to take into consideration was to adjust where the

Looking down in this view, the arrangement of the eight roof supports can be seen. Corri-Cor board has been used again for these, to give extra strength to the roof construction.

profiles all met at the centre, allowing for the thickness of the card. This was achieved by chamfering the card on the centre edge to allow the eight profiles to come together neatly at this point. With all these now cut out, they could be glued on to the base and secured at the centre join using an impact adhesive.

FITTING THE ROOF SUB-BASES

With all eight profiles now in position, the next stage was to fit all the roof sub-bases. To make sure these fitted I made templates for each panel. I used tracing paper so the edge was visible to follow with the line, and marked where it was positioned. The tracings could now be transferred on to 1.5mm mounting card, which would form the roof's sub-base. All the roof panels could now be fitted and glued into position, making sure they went on in the right order. If cut out correctly, and if time is taken at this stage, all the panels should fit up to each other.

The sub-base roofing panels cut out from a thinner card; work has now started with fixing both the upper and lower panels to the roof supports.

COVERING THE ROOF WITH SLATES

The roof was now ready to start covering with slates. Owing to this roof's unusual shape, all the slates had to be fitted individually. This also added to the rustic appearance of this fantasy-based building. All the slates were cut to a size of 3 x 8mm, with some slightly wider, measuring 4mm. The first few rows were fitted using double-sided tape attached to the card sub-base. The first row needed to overlap on the front edge by around 2mm, and when it came to the ridge or join between each section, the sides of the slates needed to be cut to follow the angle.

All the slates were now fixed on, each row overlapping the previous row by 2mm. To enhance the rustic appearance of this roof some slates were placed to overlap more, and a few by less. This practice was repeated, first working up the slope of the shallow pitch, and then following on up the steep pitch to reach the roof's pinnacle. A small amount of glue was added to the overlap to secure each slate into position.

All the roof sub-base panels are fitted, and the job of tiling it with individual tiles has now started. All the tiles were cut from greetings cards and glued on to the sub-base one by one.

The tiling can be seen here, advancing up each roof panel. The chimney stack has been built from foam board and mount card, and has been brought into position to make sure that it fitted up to the profile to the wall and to the lower pitch of the roof.

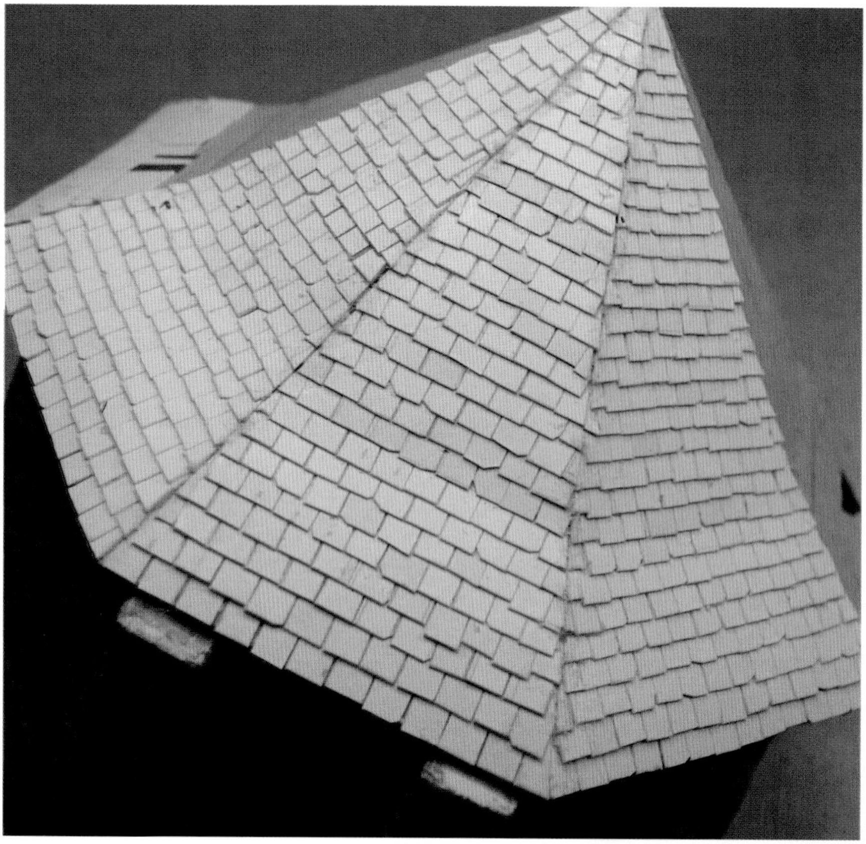

Most of the roof tiles have been fixed to the front roof panels. The tiles have been cut to follow the angle where the roof panels join together. Also some of the individual tiles have broken corners, and a few appear to have slipped down.

PAINTING THE COMPLETED ROOF

The completed roof now required painting to finish, first by using Matt Tank Grey spray paint, one of the colours available from the Humbrol Military range, which gave a good base colour. I mixed up a few more shades of grey using artist's oil paint; these were used to pick out individual slates using a 5mm chisel brush. Some of the slates were picked out in lighter shades, and some in darker ones, to give a more authentic finish to the roof.

THE STORE ROOM

The round store room is an attractive small building tapered slightly towards the top, and constructed of similar stone to the main building. However, the shallow conical roof has a covering of thatch rather than the slates of the main building. There are no windows, just a planked door for access.

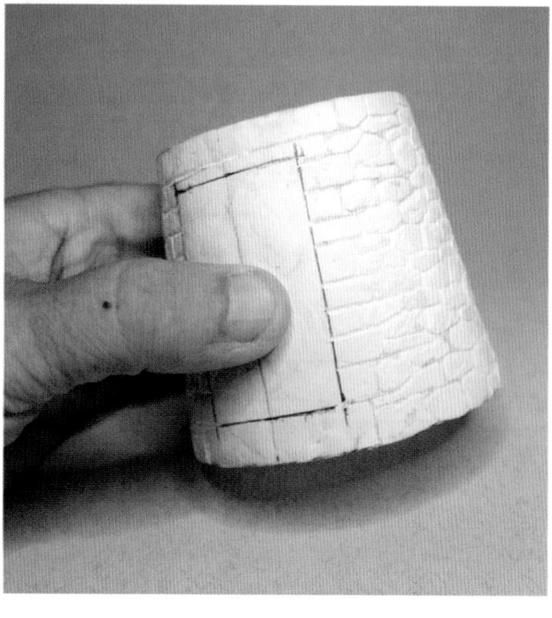

Making a start on the small tapering round store. Das modelling clay has already been added to the face of a cut-down card drinks cup.

STARTING THE MODEL

To model this unusual building I used a card coffee cup, as the tapering profile of the cup matched the tapering sides of the store room. The round footprint could be matched by cutting down the card cup and using the top half for the model. This resulted in the walls of the structure standing 3in (76mm) high at 1:48th scale.

The next task was to cut out the aperture for the store-room door, measuring 40mm deep by 30mm wide. I recommend using a sharp blade in a scalpel or hobby knife to give a clean cut through the card of the cup. You will need to be careful: score the card first, and then use a series of cuts to cut out this aperture on the curved face of the cup.

The coffee cup could now receive a skin of Das modelling clay, ready to scribe the stone masonry. The thickness of the clay would need to be the same as that applied to the main building, and scribed out using the same irregular stone pattern. I decided to paint the structure before going any further with the model. This was again matched to the stonework painted on the walls of the main building, then left to dry.

The stone masonry has been scribed out following the rubble stone used for the hovel.

The small store, alongside the hovel, showing the first painting stage: a wash to evoke the mortar colour.

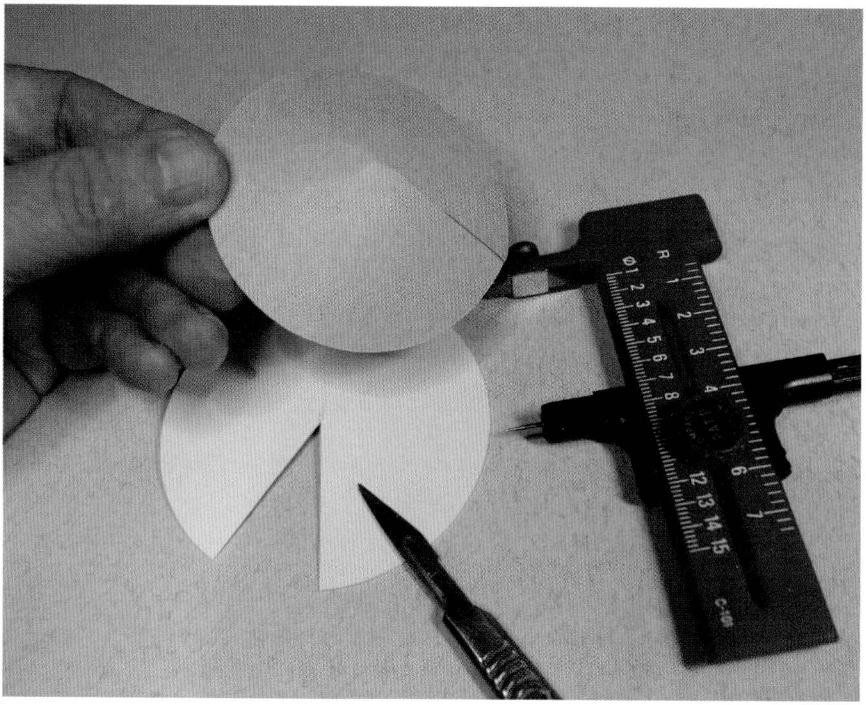

The shallow conical roof, cut from thin card using a compass cutter. A segment has been measured and cut out, and closing up the segment produces a shallow cone.

MAKING UP THE ROOF

While the paint was drying I could move on to making up the roof. This started with measuring the diameter of the top of the cup, then adding 20mm to this measurement. This was drawn out on to a piece of thin card using a compass to spin a circle. A line was drawn in from the circumference to the centre. From where this line bisected the circumference, I measured 20mm on the line of the circumference, and at this point a line was drawn back to the centre. This left me with a segment, which required cutting out, along with the marked circle. Once cut out, by closing up the cut-away segment a shallow cone is produced.

The join can now be glued and secured with masking tape or sellotape, then the coned roof can be fitted to the structure.

MAKING UP THE DOOR

The door was next to make up, using the same materials and techniques as before. The frame was added using cut-down coffee stirrers, and a door-step tread was also made. This was cut to follow the curve at the front, and cut back enough to fill in the gap at the base of the door. With this glued into position, it was coated with 'No More Cracks' to give it some surface texture.

COVERING THE ROOF WITH THATCH

The next task is to cover the roof with rough thatch, and the material chosen for this was plumber's hemp. This used to be readily available in this trade, but nowadays it is rare and hard to find. A good source, while stocks last, is from Pendon Museum, which stockpiled the material some years ago.

The hemp comes on a hank approximately 2ft (60cm) in length, and the first task is to cut it away in small bundles about 15mm long and pinched together; these are then ready to be fixed on to the card roof. A start was made with the first bundle, placing it into a bed of PVA glue and allowing it to overlap the front edge by 5mm. The next bundle was placed right next to it and fixed into place. This was now repeated until the bundles had been secured all the way round. I prefer to add more PVA at this stage, although this time it is watered down to about 50/50. This will give an extra bond by soaking through the fibres of the hemp, otherwise it can come apart on the surface.

Once this has dried sufficiently, the next course of bundles can be fixed into position. Just as with a tiled or slated roof, the bundles need to overlap the previous course. I allowed for an overlap of at least 10mm, as a reasonable depth of thatch will be required. The same process was repeated until the top was reached, with the final bundles only cut to 10mm in length.

Once all the glue had dried out, the ends were all trimmed off, including the overlapping front edge. Nail scissors were used for this, as the curved blades give a more controlled cut. I then fixed the hemp by spraying it with a light coating of hair spray.

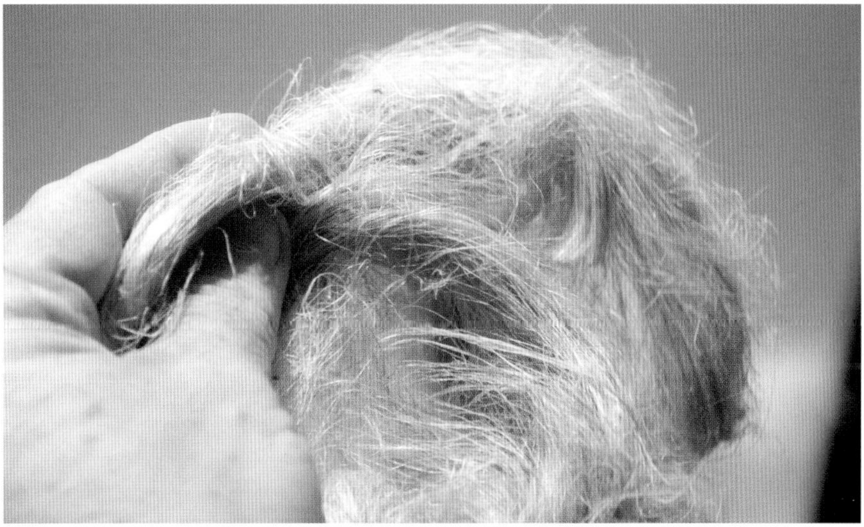

The next task was to create the thatch, which would cover this roof. Plumber's hemp is used for this, as it always gives a good representation of this roofing material.

The hemp has been pre-cut into small bundles, before being glued on using PVA.

Hairspray was used to fix the hemp fibres, before any trimming was attempted.

Trimming the thatch using nail scissors.

The thatch now neatly trimmed, and painted with a wash of Payne's grey.

PAINTING THE THATCH

To complete the thatched roof, it was painted with a thinned-down mix of oil paint. I mixed up some Payne's grey with Naples yellow added to give a worn look to the thatch. To this mix, a reasonable amount of turpentine was added, making a wash of this mixed colour. By using the paint in this way, it will soak into and through the fibres to give a realistic finish to the thatching.

CONSTRUCTING THE HOVEL'S CHIMNEY STACK

It was now time to move back to the main building, the hovel, and look at constructing its chimney stack. This needed to follow the steep angled profile of the outer wall, but remain nearly vertical, with just a slight taper towards the top. A template was made of the wall's profile, and this was transferred to a piece of 6mm foam board. The rest of the chimney stack was plotted and both sides drawn out, then cut out. The front and the rear were made from 1.5mm artist's mount card, cut to a width of 36mm. The stack was then assembled, ready for the clay to be added.

A reasonably thick skin was applied again, as the stonework needed to match the hovel. Once dry, the Das was scribed out with the larger irregular stones, although the stonework would be more regular towards the top of the stack. The rim was cut from 2mm card to a width of 8mm, before being glued to the top. I used 'No More Cracks' plaster mix again to texture the chimney's rim. It was worth painting the stack before fitting it into position up against the wall of the hovel. This was applied in exactly the same way as on the main walls, with extra retouching and weathering done after fixing.

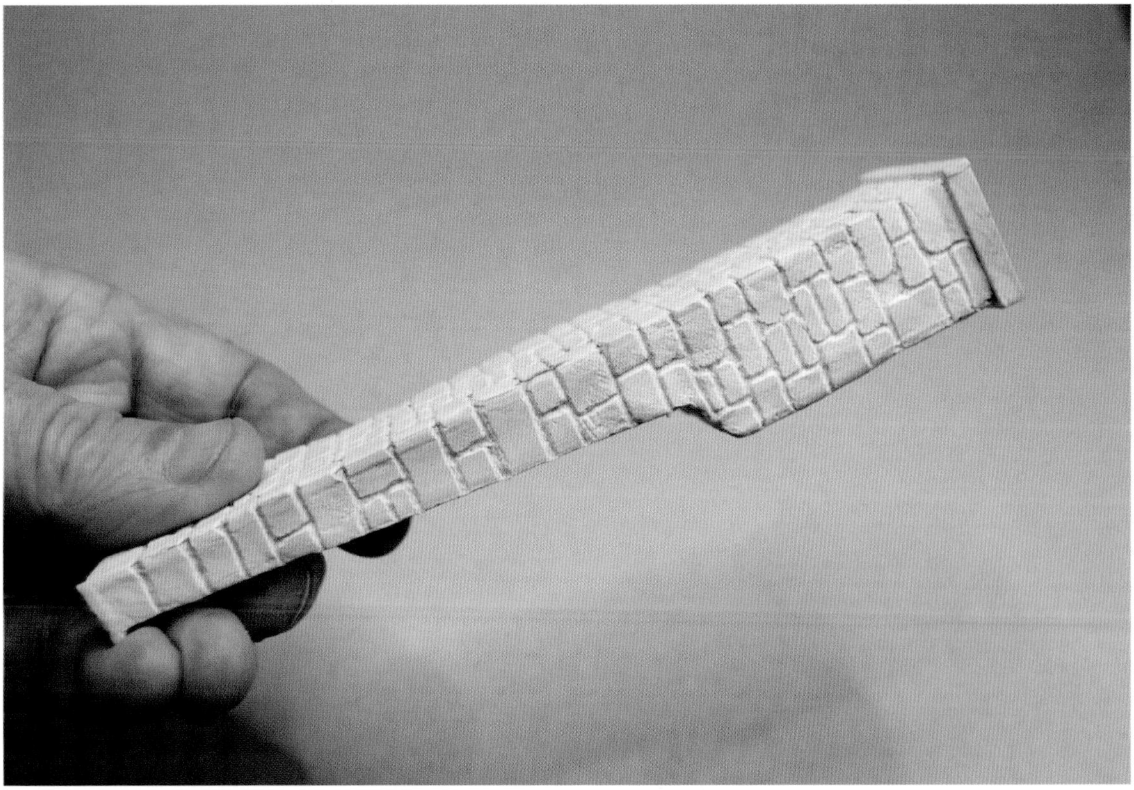

Das has been added to the faces of the chimney stack, and scribed out with the stone masonry.

THE ROCK BASE

The next task was to make up the rock plinths on which the hovel stands, raised off the ground. For the rocks I used two pieces of foam board, one piece 6mm and the other 3mm. The pieces of foam board were cut to around 30 x 25mm, then glued together face to face. Once glued, the blocks of foam board were then carved away on the facing edges using a sharp blade fitted to a scalpel or hobby knife. The method was to carve away at the edges, leaving the rocks tapering away slightly from the base.

Once happy with the rough carving, the rocks that would support the hovel could be fixed to the base

The large support stones that the hovel rests on. They are made up using different thicknesses of foam board.

Once the blocks have been made up to size, the edges are carved away.

The large support stones positioned on each of the eight corners, and fixed directly to the floor base of the hovel.

of the building. These were positioned on all the eight corners of the octagonal floor base.

With all the eight supporting rocks in position, Das modelling clay was used to add more shape and texture to the rocks. The technique was first to coat them with PVA, before adding small amounts of the clay to the faces of each rock. The clay was then sculpted using a dentist's probe or a coffee stirrer, using the reference photos to help create a good replication of the surface texture.

Then all that remained was to paint the rocks, again using photographic reference.

The support stones coated with Das modelling clay to give them an authentic textured surface.

In this closer view of the hovel, the support stones have been painted. The porch roof has also been constructed from card with edges of balsa strip, together with two laser-cut brackets or corbels fixed into position.

The round store has now been completely painted, matching the stone of the main building. The door has been made up from coffee stirrers, and painted again to match the door of the hovel. The tiles on the roof have been spray painted with the base colour of 'Matt Tank Grey' from the Humbrol military range.

FITTING THE HOVEL AND STORE ROOM TO THE SURROUNDINGS

Both the main hovel and the store room can now be married up with the ground base – a sheet of canvas board, which is a substantial, canvas-faced cardboard. The board measured 12 x 9in (305 x 229mm) and was $^{1}/_{8}$in (3mm) thick. The hovel and store room were returned and positioned roughly. I moved them around until I was satisfied with the position of both. I then marked around the base of the supporting rocks and the round store room.

With this done, both structures can be glued securely to the base using a good quality impact adhesive.

BUILDING THE STEPS TO THE FRONT DOOR

With the hovel now connected with the ground, I could build the steps to the front door; these were constructed from balsa-wood strip. The sides were measured out and cut at the required angles at both ends to fit. The steps were marked into position, then

The steps to the door have been made up using strips of balsa wood, although coffee stirrers could have been used.

a short length of a matchstick was glued to the inside of each side; this was to support each step. The steps were then cut to length, and glued on to the supporting matchsticks. Once the steps were constructed and fixed to link the ground with the front door, they could be painted. The same mix of paint as used on the door was applied to the steps, replicating the weathered, bleached finish of exterior timber.

HARD AND SOFT LANDSCAPING

This left just the finishes to be made to all the surrounding ground, including any hard and soft landscaping. In fact there wasn't too much hard landscaping, just a few cobbles and flagstones required. The rest would be soft landscaping, mainly consisting of grasses and a few weeds.

The hovel and the store have now been temporarily placed in position on the baseboard. Das has been put down in the areas that will form the hard standing.

Painting the ground colour on the rest of the baseboard, but leaving the hard standing unpainted. Note that some of the roofing tiles have been picked out in lighter and darker shades of the grey.

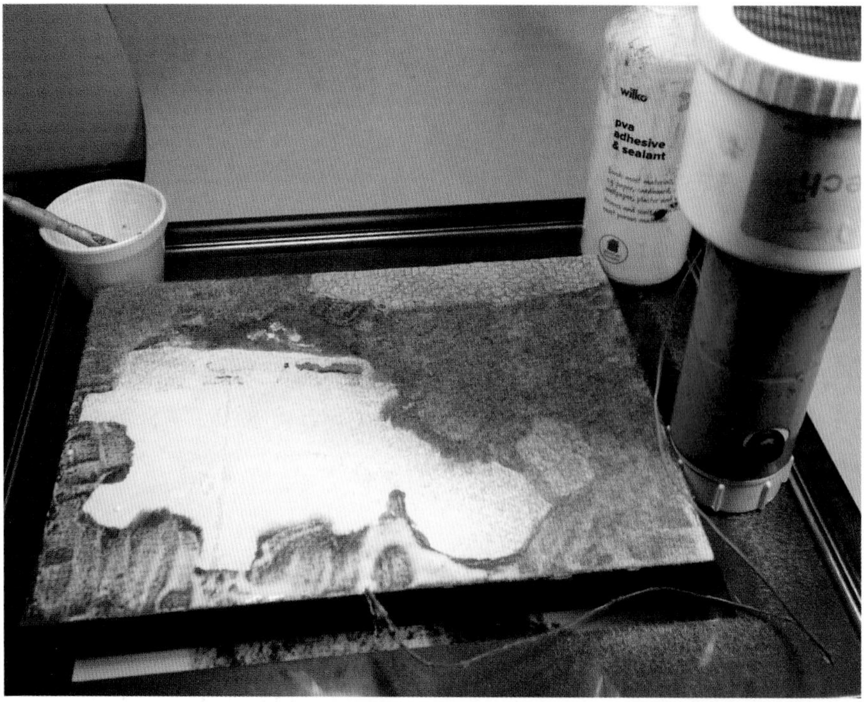

The hovel and store have both been removed so the ground can be grassed over. Short, static fibres have been selected from the 'Greenscene' range, and applied into a coat of PVA using a static grass applicator.

Both hovel and store fixed firmly in position. The roof of the porch has now been painted, and the cobbles on the pathway, together with the flagstones around the doors, have all been scribed out.

Starting with the hard landscaping, Das was first put down in front of the steps and the door to the storeroom. This was scribed out when dry to form the cobbles of the path and the flagstones immediately outside the store-room door. These were painted in more or less the same shades as were used for the masonry of both structures.

With this done and the paint dry, the rest of the ground was tackled, first painting in the earth colour mixed from Payne's grey and yellow ochre, although this time using acrylic paint. This of course dries much more quickly than oil paint, and allowed for the area to be grassed over within ten minutes. I used static grass fibres again, selecting a few shades of green together with straw. A liberal coat of PVA was applied to the desired areas before using the static grass applicator. I also added some foam flock from 'Woodland Scenics', scattering it in areas close to the hovel, using spray glue to fix it into position.

ADDING THE DRESSINGS AND FINISHES

To finish this imaginary building and setting, a few dressings were needed to really set the model off.

The variety of pots and pans along with the rustic table found outside the prototype hovel at Blists Hill – valuable reference when it came to dressing out this model.

A number of interesting dressings found while visiting a dolls' house fair. These were all painted using the 'supa-matt' acrylic paints from 'Omen Miniatures'. These accessories were slightly out of scale, but the larger size fitted in well with this fantasy-based model.

My thinking here was to look for some out-of-scale dressings of curiosity to create a fantasy setting. I managed to find a few items while visiting a dolls' house fair, which were intended for 1:24th scale scenes. These included a number of baskets, plant pots and pumpkins, which were ideal. The latter would be especially appropriate to dress out the setting for this model. I also looked at adding some scale items such as a barrow, a number of beer crates and a wood pile. All these dressings would be placed in groups to make them look more authentic – if you are not sure, look for photographic reference of old cottage gardens.

This brings this fantasy model project to a conclusion. The building's unusual shape created a modelling challenge, but the finished result made

The model nearing completion, with the various dressings placed just outside the hovel, dominated by giant pumpkins.

A couple of logs used to dress this side of the model. These utilized broken pieces of small branches picked up on a country walk.

To finish the roof and to make the hovel look more rustic, some lichen growth was added. The yellow grass-coloured fine turf from 'Woodland Scenics' was used for this.

The finished model of the gamekeeper's hovel.

it all worthwhile, and I am sure it is something a model maker with reasonable skills would be able to take on. It could also be scaled down to a smaller size to fit into a larger school of wizardry-themed fantasy layout or diorama. I have purposely included a plan and concept artwork to show what might be achieved if modellers want to follow up this idea to completion in Chapter 6.

CHAPTER FIVE

'RAVEN'S RAVINE': BUILDING A SMALL LAYOUT DIORAMA

The project in this chapter shows how to build a small table-top diorama. The concept was to create a model railway that would run through a dramatic rocky terrain, but would also feature interesting structures, such as the remains of castle towers, standing stones, follies, and the ruins of an abbey. The centrepiece would consist of a rocky ravine, with a river cascading over high waterfalls. The ravine would be crossed by three bridges, the lowest and the middle bridge of ancient medieval origins, while the highest span would be a Victorian cast-iron arched bridge to carry the narrow-gauge railway, high above the river below.

Creating a more fantasy-themed layout will hopefully appeal to the younger modeller, as images of castles have always sparked a child's imagination. This project would be ideal for a father or grandfather to build along with their children or grandchildren. In our modern world there are too many other interactive high-tech alternatives that grab the attention of the younger generation, and this is a shame, as model making can be so beneficial to developing hands-on skills, as well as developing and feeding a creative young mind.

The planning of this fantasy-based layout needed to incorporate prototypical structures as well as a scenic terrain. These can be used in their entirety, or just parts selected, to fit in with the desired finished diorama. Thus, as when planning any model railway or model diorama, research comes to the fore, and by searching through books or on the internet, structures and dramatic landscape features were found that would fit nicely into this project. I purposely chose a selection of structures and scenic features that could be found within the UK, and most were not too far away to plan a visit.

ASSEMBLING RESEARCH INFORMATION

The research part of model making I find quite exciting and informative. For this model I needed to find buildings, and in particular castles, preferably in a ruined state. I also wanted to feature an abbey in ruins, and interesting-looking follies, again either intact or in ruins. A number of old bridges were selected that would fit into the scene, as well as a group of ancient standing stones. My research would also extend to finding locations to suit the project's landscaping requirements, where dramatic rock formations dominated, and actual ravines where a number of fast-flowing streams have cut through the terrain. I already had a few locations in mind, and I was sure these could all be found within the British Isles.

We are blessed nowadays to have the internet as a tool for research, but don't forget books can also be of use. I have found 'Wikipedia' most helpful when searching on the internet, and image libraries can give instant visual results, although unfortunately they don't always give a location.

Once suitable subjects and locations have been found, it is strongly recommended that you visit them in person, as you can't beat experiencing the real location. Making a site visit will give a true sense of scale, something that a photograph or film will not be able to give. Being at the location will also give you the chance to take photographs for yourself of the features at different angles, including a few close-ups – all valuable information to use later when producing the model.

Taking measurements will also be very helpful, though if this is not practical, then try to estimate measurements by making sketches and noting them down while on site. Take photographs to record how

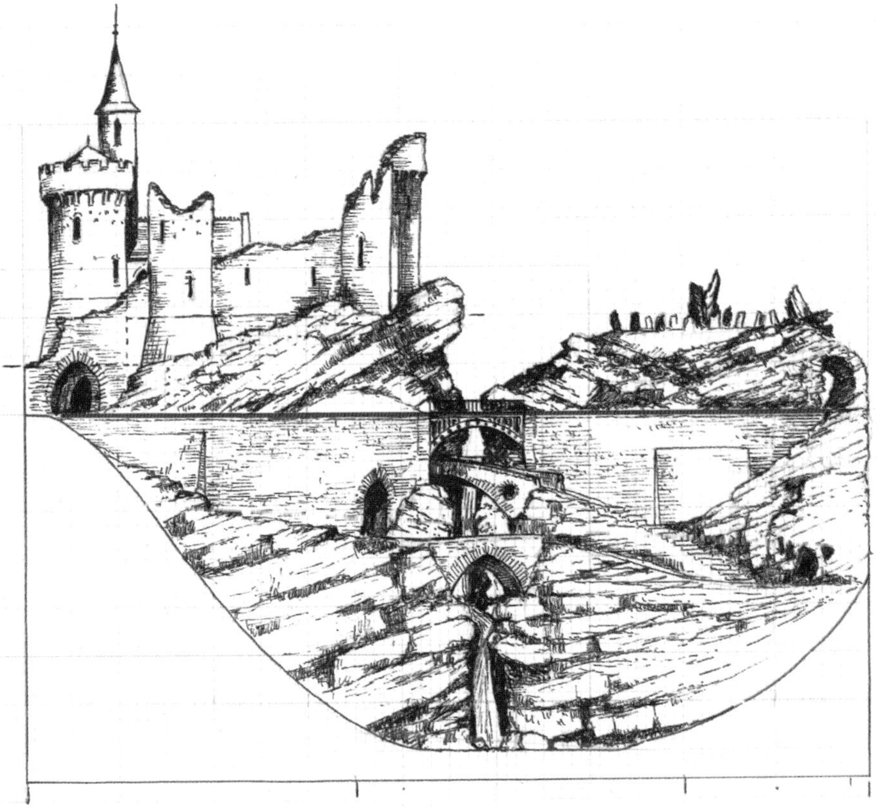

The original concept artwork produced for 'Raven's Ravine', in which a partially ruined castle dominates the left-hand side.

the elements have affected buildings and structures, and most importantly all the landscape features. The more visual information that you can gather together on site, the better chance you will have of producing convincing models.

Always take a digital camera on location, together with a notebook and pen. If you intend to make rough drawings on site, then A4 sheets of graph paper, a clipboard, pencil and eraser will also be needed. If you can take measurements on site safely, then a long and a short tape measure will be required. A sighting pole is always very useful when estimating heights: this is simple to make, from a broom handle painted white, with bands of bright colour paint measured out at certain intervals.

Once the research information has been found, it is wise to put it all together in a portfolio that can be used at the next stage, which will be creating a plan.

DRAWING THE PLAN

Start by setting out all the information you have collected on site, ready to start your plan. To begin with, this will involve producing rough drawings that include everything you wish to feature on your model layout or diorama. A certain amount of discipline will be needed in deciding how all the elements will come together in a practical way, so they look visually correct. Often this element of control is overlooked at this stage, with modellers sometimes trying to cram too much into the available space, which will result in the model looking totally 'overdone'. Try and plan this out on paper, making a few alternatives, until you arrive at the best solution.

The next stage is to re-draw this plan to the desired scale, starting with the baseboard. Next, draw in the course of the railway track, once this has been plotted, then fit everything from the rough

After visiting 'Hawkstone Park Follies' in Shropshire, I was inspired by the ruins of 'Red Castle' and thought it would be interesting to introduce them to 'Raven's Ravine'. This led me to draw up a second version of concept artwork with the ruins of the towers included, but combined with a fantasy castle. A folly was also added on the right to balance out the composition.

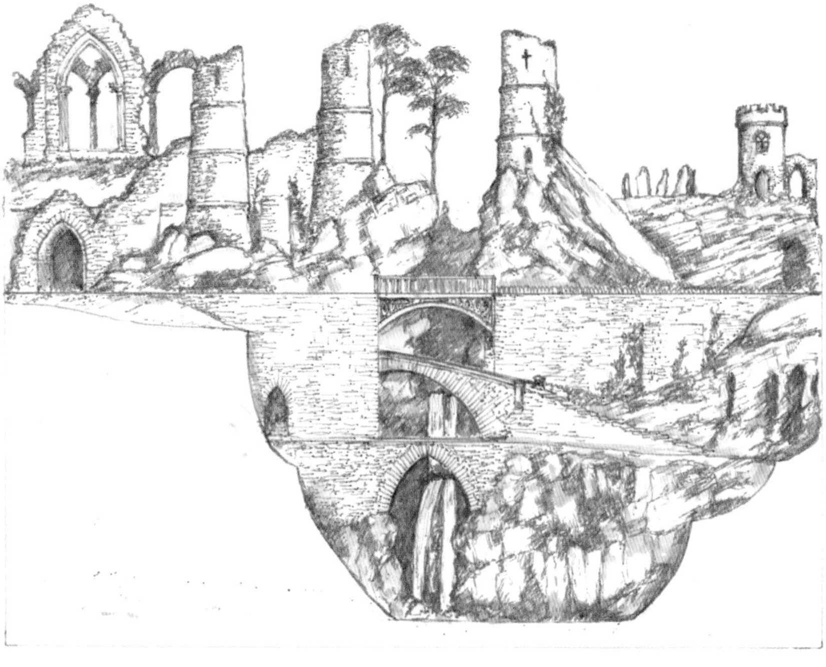

A third concept artwork was drawn up, this time substituting the fantasy castle for the ruins of a monastic abbey, the inspiration for which came from seeing various paintings from the picturesque period. This version of 'Raven's Ravine' would also feature 'Old John' folly above the standing stones on the right. The abbey ruins have been left as a removable section of the model, so the fantasy castle could be made and used as an alternative in the future.

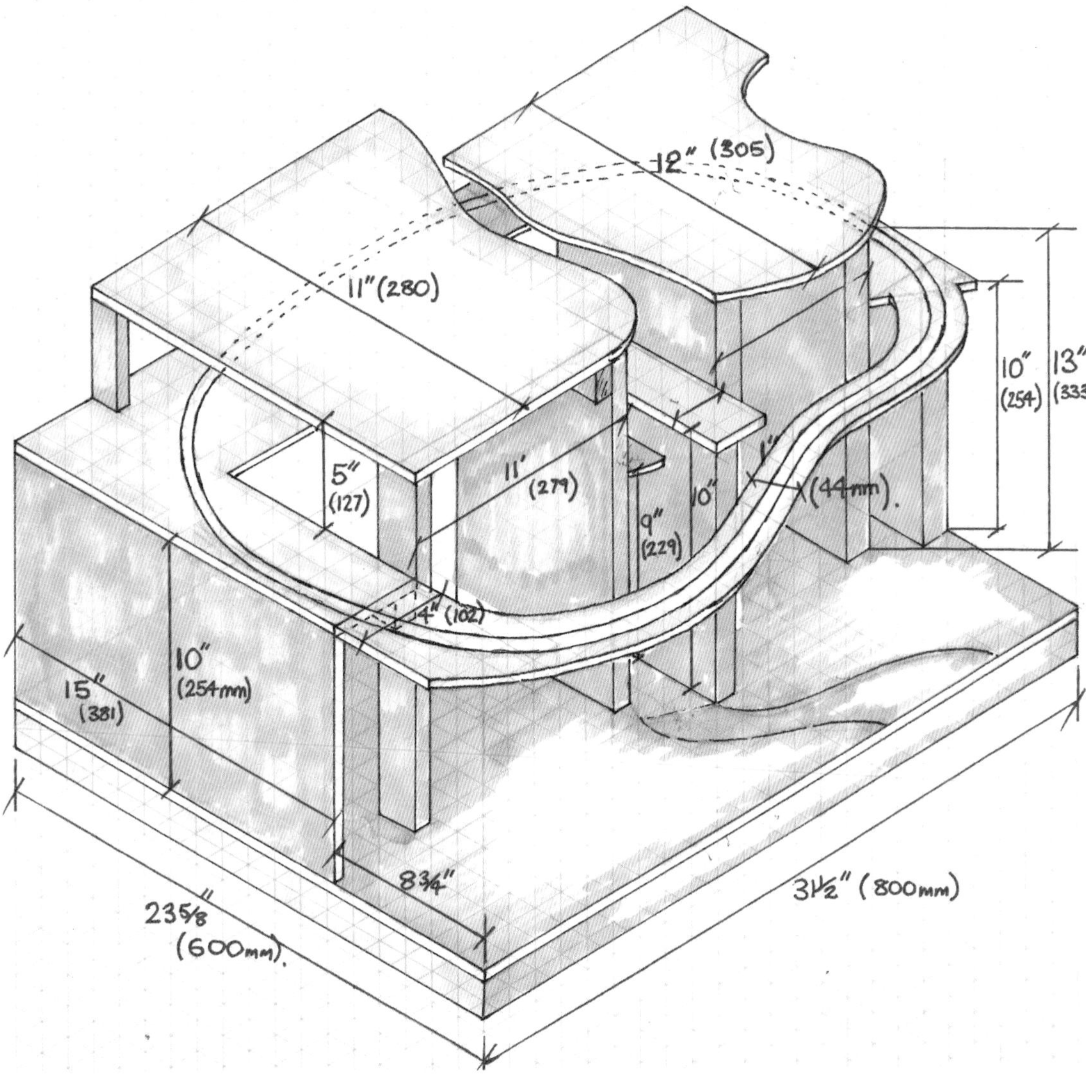

Before any construction started it was decided to plan out all the different levels involved in building this model diorama. The result is seen with measurements added, all to make construction as straightforward as possible.

sketch to this, but this time to scale. You might find that adjustments have to be made, although if the original sketch has taken scale into consideration then everything should slot into place. It is important always to produce an accurate scale plan first, then construction should not throw up any major problems – although inevitably you will have to make a few slight adjustments, as seeing it flat on paper is not the same as seeing a three-dimensional version. If, however, you have access to CAD, then this could give you the three-dimensional option.

If you don't have this facility, then another scale drawing would help construction – though this time the plan would show the levels required for this model, with the track bed of the railway being the most important. Once this has been established, then

A selection of packaging including various cardboard roll centres and postal tubes, and a number of polystyrene and plastic tubs. Most of these were used for the construction of castle towers on 'Ravens Ravine'.

Some of the adhesives and filler plaster used to construct the model structures and scenic features on 'Raven's Ravine'.

all the other levels can be plotted, with the river at the bottom of the falls at the lowest, through to the base of the abbey ruins at the highest.

The main concept for this model diorama was to build upwards from the baseboard, creating a more scenic result. This will give more depth to the model and will look far more pleasing visually. To see how this would appear, I decided to go one stage further from the flat plans, and made an illustration. By doing this, you should see just how the finished model will appear. Another way is to make a scaled-down mock-up. This might seem to be a lot of unnecessary extra work, but it is well worth the effort. Nor should it cost too much, as a quick mock-up can be made from corrugated carton board.

MAKING A START ON CONSTRUCTION

MAKING UP THE BASEBOARD

The main foundation for this small layout – and for that matter any other layout or diorama – will be some kind of baseboard. Baseboards can be made up as open framed or solid topped. The baseboard

A model diorama such as this has to start with a baseboard. I found a stretched canvas on a substantial frame in a local charity shop. It was just about the right size, making it ideal to build this model on, although extra stretchers had to be added to give extra strength.

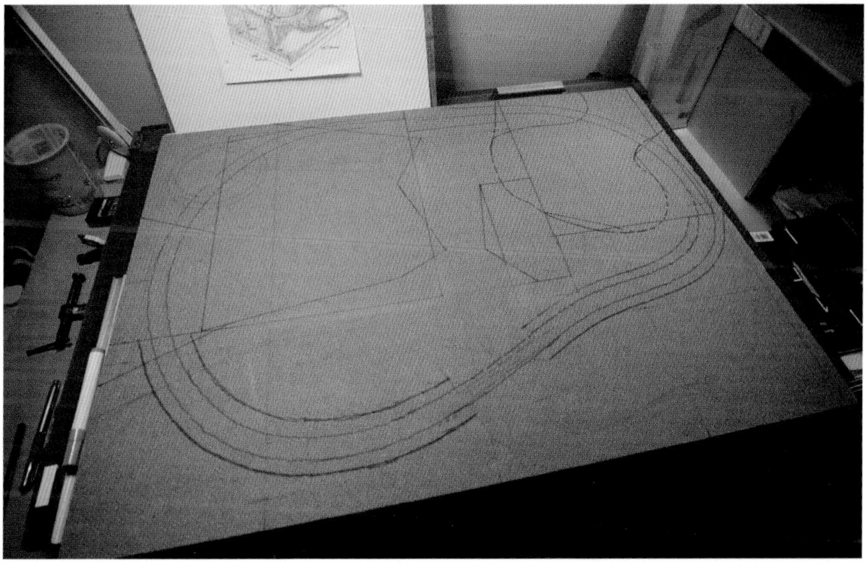

The face was covered with a sheet of lightweight insulation board, which is used as the foundation for putting down laminated flooring. The plan has been drawn out on the surface to guide with construction.

for this project would need to be strong and rigid, but at the same time as light as possible. My original plan was for a baseboard measuring 30 x 24in (762 x 610mm); however, while visiting a charity shop I found a stretched canvas picture, supported on a substantial wooden frame. This frame, although rigid, appeared to be very light, just what I was looking for, and it only cost me £3! It's always worth looking out in charity shops or at car boot sales for items that can be used directly, or can be easily converted for model-making use.

This picture measured 31 x $23^5/_8$in (800 x 600mm), so not too far away from what I had originally planned. The 1 x 1in (25 x 25mm) framing provided for this picture was ideal. However, the canvas was not going to be strong enough to rely on for the baseboard top, so I needed to create a top for the frame using something more substantial. To keep the construction light, I selected a sheet of flooring insulation board, its intended use to be put down as a foundation for laminated flooring.

I could have removed the canvas from the framing altogether, but I decided to keep the canvas on and glue the insulation board to it. I then made this connection more secure by adding a number of panel pins, hammering them in all the way through the boarding and into the framing underneath. The insulation board was larger than the frame on one side, so trimming was required after the glue had completely bonded.

This made a reasonable baseboard top, but because the material is so light, there was some movement in the central area. This needed to be addressed, of course, and was easily remedied by adding three cross-members or stretchers on the underside. I matched the timber used on the frame for this, cutting three lengths, positioning one across the centre and two equally spaced on each side. Turning the baseboard over I tested the centre area again to make sure this annoying bounce had been cured.

TRANSFERRING THE TRACK TO THE BASEBOARD

Before any construction was attempted, the course of the track needs to be transferred to the baseboard first. The best way to do this is to use the actual track, in this case a length of the 009, flexible narrow-gauge track. To achieve the course required, the length would need to be gently pushed and shaped to give all the sharp curves. While holding the track in position it can be temporarily pinned down. I found that this was best done by splitting this exercise into two halves. Once the curves of the track course have been achieved on one half, use a felt-tipped pen to mark along the outside edge of the sleepers. Lift the track away again, and repeat the exercise on the other half, lifting the track to leave the marked-out course of the track on the baseboard, acting as your track template.

The marked-out course of the track can now be traced on to an A2 sheet of tracing paper or any semi-transparent material. This can be now put on one side for use later to plot out the track again in the final elevated position. It was much easier to carry this out on the flat baseboard first, than struggling with this when it comes to constructing the higher level.

BUILDING UP THE HIGHER LEVEL

Attention can now be concentrated on building up this higher level. The main priority was to make this layout as light as possible during all stages of

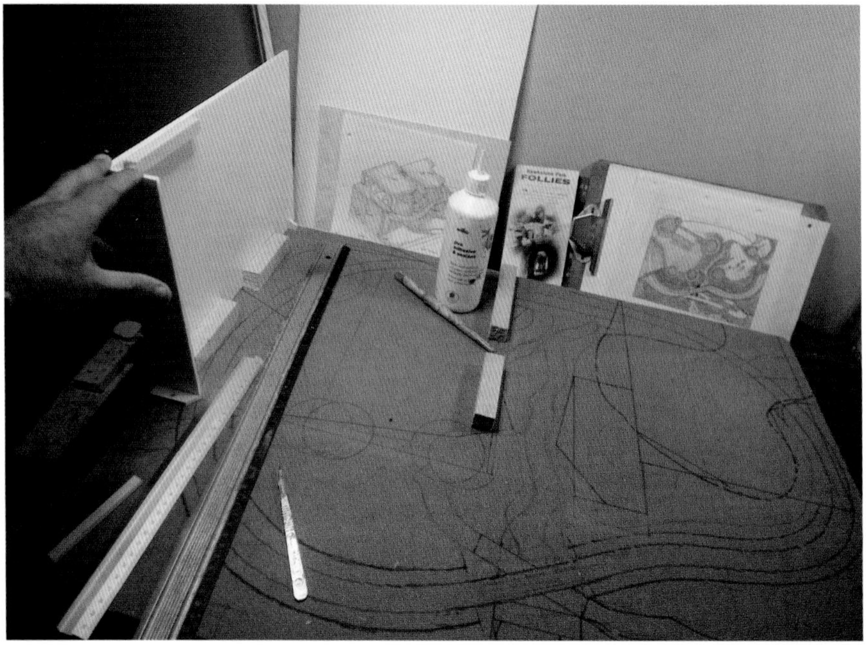

The upper level is being built up from 6mm foam board, with 25 x 25mm balsa wood used to secure the join with the baseboard.

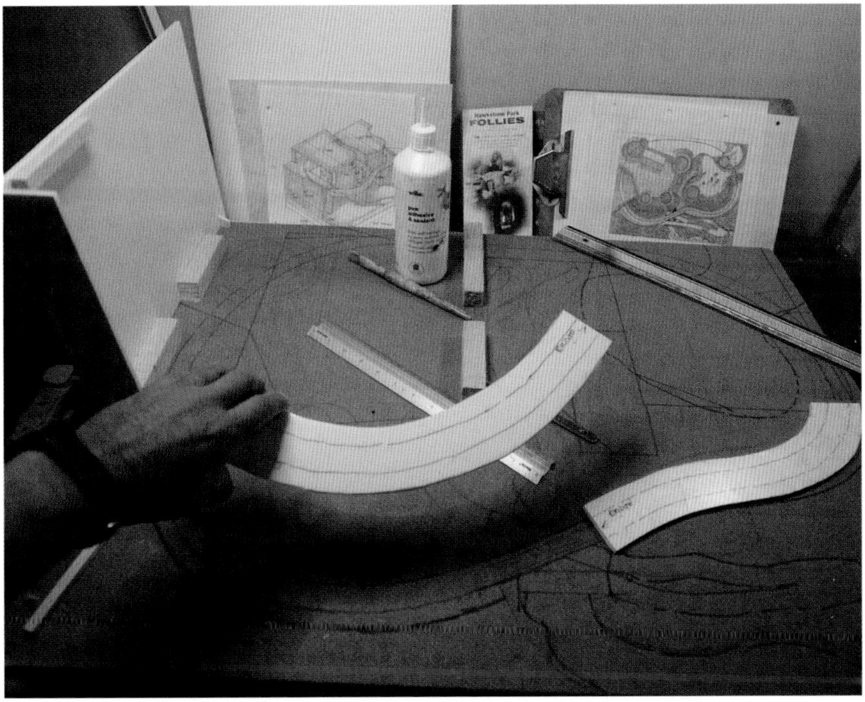

The track bases already cut out to extend the track on the front part of the diorama. These will take the narrow-gauge railway over the elevated stone embankments and over the ravine.

construction, so I decided to use 6mm foam board instead of plywood. Measurements were taken, then a full side panel and part facing panels were cut to size and glued into position; the panels were secured with blocks of balsa wood glued to the baseboard. Balsa wood was also used for the stretcher braces to support the tops, again using the 6mm foam board to fabricate the actual tops.

CONSTRUCTING THE RAVINE

Work now concentrated on the ravine. The first stage was to build up a level using foam board to form the higher bed of the river. This would be in an elevated position in the centre of the model, raised on a few balsa wood risers. Once the river bed was in position, then the rock faces to the ravine could be constructed; I selected the insulation foam (Styrofoam) used in the building trade for this task. First this was cut to reasonable sized chunks and glued in position along the sides of the river bed.

The Styrofoam can now be carved to shape, using photographs of appropriate rock faces and strata. An old bread knife was ideal for this task, although any fine-tooth saw would also do the job. Although the surface of the Styrofoam gave a reasonable replication of the texture of the rock, I decided to paint on some 'No More Cracks' plaster filler – this gave a more convincing texture due to its gritty finish.

Once the plaster had dried, paint was applied, first using a mix of Payne's grey and yellow ochre acrylic paint. This made a good base colour as it was a good replication of the dark weathered shades of the sandstone or gritstone. When dry, artist's oil paints were then used to create the natural highlight colours of the stone. Reference photographs taken at Hawkstone Park and Lumsdale were used to match the colours as accurately as possible, especially those in the shady and wet areas of the ravine. This would be most evident on the cliff face at the rear of the waterfall. The material used here was a mixture of cork bark and chunks of polystyrene packaging. The face of the polystyrene was broken before being coated with the plaster mix.

When this had been painted, the highlights and lighter shades of the sandstone needed to be added. The best way of achieving this is to dry brush oil paint using a mix of burnt umber, yellow ochre and

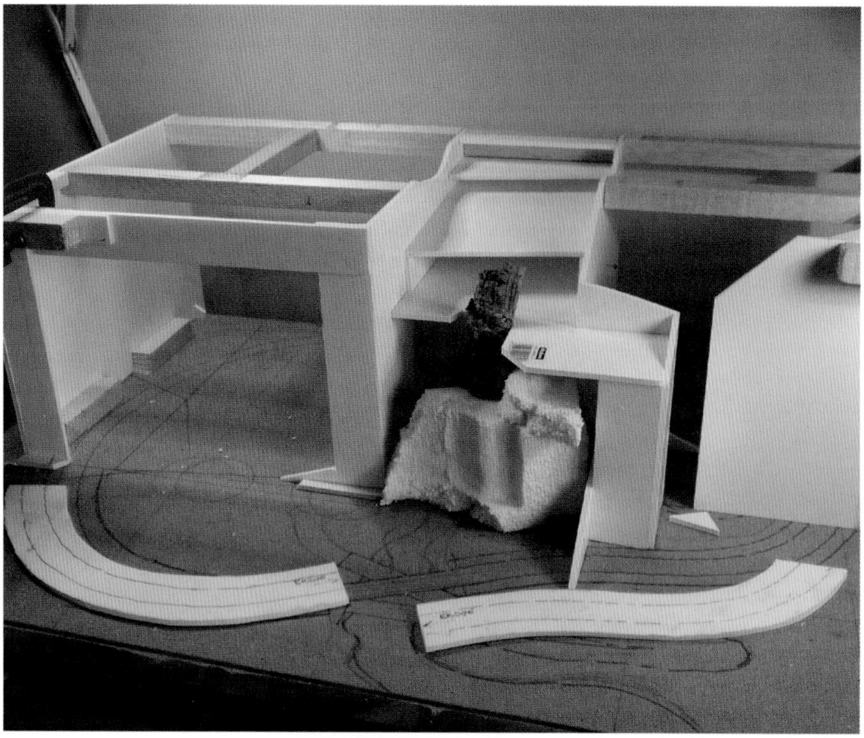

The rear of the model is taking shape, with the high level built from foam board. Note the gap left in the central area where the levels are being put in for the river, and the high waterfall at the front.

The high levels have been built up, and the levels for the river bed can clearly be seen. At the front the foam board has been cut away in readiness for the scenery to be built up. Note the marking out has been pre-drawn on the baseboard. This included the track bed, which was traced from this before being cut out ready to be placed into position at a later stage.

titanium white. Try stippling the paint to the surface using a 4mm filbert brush to give the best results.

Once this was done, a start could be made on constructing the waterfall.

THE WATERFALL

I looked at various materials to create the waterfall, before selecting the nylon fibres supplied by 'Deluxe Materials'. The fibres needed to be teased away from the pack and then combed through, in order to keep them all 'flowing' in one direction. This would give a reasonable impression of the falling water, although I was not totally convinced with just using the fibres alone. The combed fibres were glued to the top lip of the rock face and stretched to reach the bottom, where they were glued again.

However, I wanted to make the fibres more convincing in replicating the falling water. This was achieved by first lightly spraying the fibres with an artist's fixative spray, then applying titanium white oil paint, brushed on lightly. To finish, gloss varnish was added, to give the sparkle required. This combination

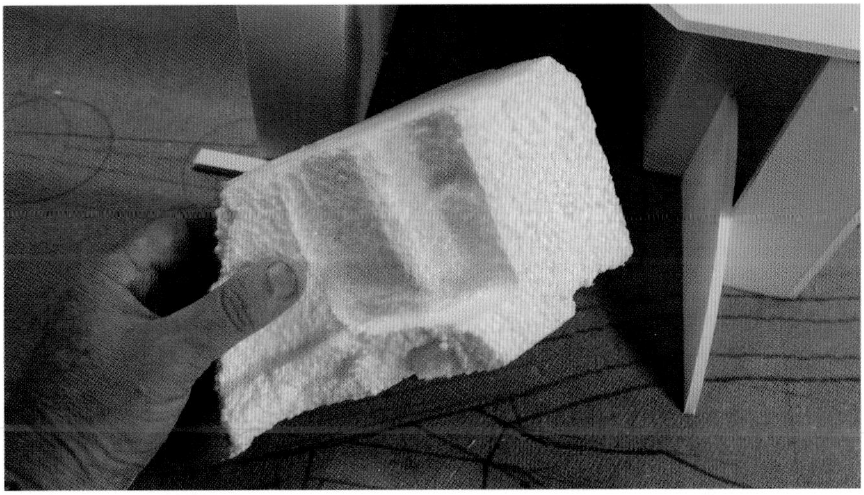

The first stage of creating the scenery, using polystyrene packaging to make up the rock face immediately behind the lower part of the waterfall.

The cliff face behind the waterfall is now progressing, with cork bark added above the broken-faced polystyrene packaging.

Building up the first stage of the ravine using insulation foam. This has been roughly carved from blocks of the foam.

The rocky ravine progressing well, with the foam now carved and shaped. At this stage the foam has been coated with PVA to seal it, before a coat of 'No More Cracks' is added to give the rocks some texture.

The rock face ledges immediately behind the waterfall are being sculpted using a palette knife, although an old kitchen knife can be used. To the left, an old bread knife has been used to cut and carve away the insulation foam.

Prototype inspiration was found for the rocky ravine at Hawkstone Park in Shropshire: the dramatic windswept rock face known as the 'Awful Precipice'.

More prototype inspiration was found when visiting the Light Spout Waterfall on the Long Mynd. This natural feature provided an ideal reference when it came to constructing the waterfall for our model.

The waterfall was started by using the product 'Scenic Fibres' from the 'Deluxe Materials' range. These fibres were lightly combed in the direction of the falling water, then carefully glued into position. Note that before the waterfall was attempted, all the rock face behind had to be painted and weathered first.

To make the waterfall look more authentic, first the fibres were sprayed with a fixative spray, then a combination of white oil paint and clear varnish was lightly brushed over them. The effect of this was to make the fibres glisten when the light caught them, and this gave a very convincing representation of the falling water.

certainly gave the effect I was looking for, and I was totally satisfied with the result.

The deep water at the foot of the waterfall was created by painting a base coat of dark green, then adding two coats of clear gloss varnish. Also required was an evocation of the splashing and torrents of white water created by the force of the falling water; most of this was formed for the model by using a mixture of PVA and 'Power Bond Adhesive' from 'Wilko's', with white oil paint added to finish.

With the waterfall complete, along with the rock formations behind and those forming the steep sides to the ravine, we can now proceed with constructing the track bed of the railway.

CREATING THE TRACK BED OF THE RAILWAY

The track bed can now be addressed by again using 6mm foam board. This is where the tracing made earlier comes to the fore: by taping the tracing down over the foam board the outline can easily be cut out. This will give the two sections of the track bed, ready to be fixed into the final raised position. To raise the track bed a number of risers would be required. These were cut to size using both 6mm foam board and 3mm balsa wood, with the foam board reserved to form the abutments of the top bridge.

LAYING THE TRACK

Once the track bed has been glued and secured to all the risers, the Peco 009 narrow-gauge track can be laid. This type, known as 'crazy track', was ideal for this project, although extra breaks had to be cut in the sleeper webs to allow the rails to be curved to the very tight radii required. The track was then pinned and secured to the track bed. A short section of track was cut to span the gap, and was then connected to the rest, completing the circuit. This short section would eventually be glued to a decking of the bridge.

Before moving on to the next stage, I decided to ballast the track, which would secure it even more firmly to the track bed. I used a selection of fine-grain ballast and sand, which was lightly scattered over the

With the waterfall now complete and the area around the ravine all painted and weathered, work started on assembling the track bed on the left-hand side. This has now been fixed into its elevated position on a series of supports, made from 6mm foam board and balsa wood. Polystyrene packaging has again been used to fill in behind the track bed.

On the left-hand side of the diorama the 009 'Crazy Track' has been laid. Track pins have been used initially to fix down the track, with the plastic sleepers drilled first.

Looking up at the elevated track bed, the model has moved on somewhat. The right-hand side has now been built up with the track laid on to it. The ornate iron bridge to take the railway over the ravine has been fixed in, and preparations are being made to ballast the track. The profile arch of the higher packhorse bridge has been brought in and positioned on an abutment made from foam board.

The same stage, looking down on the progress made. The track is being ballasted, using a mix of fine graded grit and sand.

track. This was then dampened using a garden mister spray, and then dilute PVA was added using an eye dropper. This would flow between the grains of the ballast, bonding this and the track to the bed. Small amounts of washing-up liquid were added to the PVA, to avoid creating any surface tension. The ballasted track was now left to dry completely, then track and ballast were spray painted using 'Matt Tank Grey' from the Humbrol military aerosol range.

THE ROCK FACES ABOVE THE WATERFALL

The next stage was to concentrate on the centre area again, and decide where the three bridges would be positioned. However, before this the rock faces above the waterfall would need to be addressed, as it would be difficult to work on them once the bridges were fixed in position. I selected more blocks of insulation foam for this, which were roughly carved using an old bread knife. More detailed carving was then executed to replicate the ridges in this type of sandstone. When gluing the carved block in place a good tip is to push through plastic or wooden cocktail sticks as well, as this will give extra reinforcement to the joins.

CONSTRUCTING THE THREE BRIDGES

FITTING THE TOP BRIDGE

The abutments could now be fitted for the highest bridge, which would carry the railway. Foam board was used initially, with extra mounting card added to the face. This was then coated with a thin skin of Das modelling clay. (Remember, the more you wet the clay, the thinner the coat that will be achieved.) Once the clay had dried on both abutments it would be scribed, creating the stone masonry.

With the track complete and the abutments in place, the top bridge to carry the railway could be

In this very low angle photograph, the top railway bridge is now fixed. Only at this stage has the higher-level packhorse bridge been placed in position. This bridge is nearing completion, with the side profiles, decking and the underside of the arch all assembled together. The next stage was to completely cover the structure with Das modelling clay, and to scribe it out so as to represent masonry. However, to do this the bridge would have to be removed again.

fitted. I found that the Victorian iron arched bridge supplied by 'Wills' was perfect in appearance and span, although the bridge deck had to be fabricated to fit the gap. This was constructed using a combination of styrene planking, again from the 'Wills' range, and balsa wood strip.

THE HIGHER PACKHORSE BRIDGE

The two lower bridges, both packhorse bridges, would have been constructed from stone. The higher one of the two consisted of a single sweeping arch spanning the gorge, with the deck rising on a gradual incline. The lower bridge featured a single Gothic arch and would have been of medieval origin. It was based on the lower bridge at Devil's Bridge in mid-Wales.

The prototype spans at Devil's Bridge gave me the idea to make this the main feature and focal point for this model. The position of the three bridges was critical: I wanted them to span the gorge on different levels, and also to cross it at slightly different angles, giving the effect of interlacing with each other.

Card was chosen as the main material for both bridges. The gap was first measured, then a simple cardboard mock-up made; this would be used as a template for the actual model. The two profiles were marked and cut out, first making sure the sweeping arch was correct. Then the curving, inclined deck and the inside of the arch were constructed, and stretcher sections were cut to fit between the two sides.

Both the inside of the arch and the deck were fixed to the sides using a number of balsa wood blocks: these were positioned and glued to the sides, following the curve of the arch and the inclined curve of the deck. To make the inside of the arch, a thinner card was used, which would curve easily by running it through the fingers. The same card was also used for the deck, and curved using the same method.

Once the glue had bonded, the stretcher sections were glued in, making a rigid structure ready for the next stage, which was to add a skin of Das modelling clay: this would form all the masonry. However, the inside of the arch was coated with a mix of PVA and 'No More Cracks' from 'Unibond'. This would create the required texture, and also add extra strength to the construction. Before scribing out, I decided first of all to pencil in the radiating pattern of the voussoirs, making sure they looked correct.

The scribing could now begin, starting with the long voussoirs that made up the sweeping arch. This would be a major feature of this unique bridge, and would make it visually appealing. Once the scribing was completed the structure could be positioned with the deep side connected to an abutment, and the other side fitting snuggly into the rock face of the ravine.

THE LOWER PACKHORSE BRIDGE

Work could now begin on the lower bridge, using the same materials. This bridge would be at the same level on each side, and have a level deck. A Gothic arch would span the gorge, and would have to be plotted using a curved template. I used a tea plate, which was ideal for the two curves required. It was important to make sure the arch was plotted correctly by first measuring the span, dividing this to find the centre, and then marking in the vertical centre line. Next, the height of the arch was measured and marked in. Once this had been determined the curves could be plotted, bringing them together to a point at the apex.

The construction method was more or less the same as the first packhorse bridge, though the inside of the arch this time required a fold in order to follow the shape of the Gothic pointed arch. This bridge also featured low parapet walls topped with coping stones. Two balsa wood strips were used to fabricate these.

Once construction was completed, the structure was coated with a thin skin of Das modelling clay on the facing sides, and 'No More Cracks' plaster mix was brushed on to the inside of the arch and again on the coping stones topping the low parapets.

One additional feature to this bridge was the placing of protruding stones following the curves of the Gothic arch. I used small cut pieces of card for these, which were carefully cut into the skin and secured with glue. I then brushed on a mix of PVA and 'No More Cracks' to give them a convincing stone-like finish.

The scribing followed a similar pattern to the previous bridge, but this time the voussoirs were not as long, and interconnected with the horizontal coursing. This bridge arch connected with the tall stone abutments on each side. The abutments also needed to be covered with a skin of Das, and then scribed with the level stone coursing. This extended from both the inside facing walls to the walls on each side of the arch. The facing stonework of the lower abutments had to merge seamlessly into the rugged rock faces towering high above the river.

In this low angle view, both the higher and lower packhorse bridges have been completed, including painting and weathering, and fitting them up to their abutments. The abutments have also been faced with clay, which has been scribed out so the masonry effect matches the two bridges.

This lower packhorse bridge would be the nearest to the front of the diorama as well as being aligned with the front of the baseboard. The two higher bridges would both be positioned at slight angles to the front, and both are set further back.

I painted the two stone bridges once they had been glued and secured to the abutments and rock faces. First a wash of light grey oil paint was applied all over, allowing it to run into all the scribed-out gaps between the stonework. Once this had dried, a mix of Payne's grey and burnt umber was dry brushed over the surface of the stones, representing the slate used to construct the two bridges. Highlights to the stone were added later by dry brushing a little titanium white over the face. Some highlights were applied by using my fingers – you don't always have to use a brush!

CONSTRUCTING THE STONE EMBANKMENT WALLS

The abutments were tackled next, using exactly the same painting techniques. Construction of the high embankment was started by adding a series of supporting strips. I used balsa wood for this to keep the construction light, cutting 3mm balsa wood into strips measuring 15mm wide and cut to the depth of the embankment. The strips were then spaced out roughly 30mm apart, and glued to the baseboard and to the underneath of the foam-board track bed. To secure the strips to the base I added blocks of balsa measuring 10 x 10mm, just to give some extra support.

The strips acted as backing for the facing walls, which were made from cereal packet card, as this could be curved easily to the follow the path of the track bed. The card was cut to size and glued to the supporting strips to give a strong, lightweight structure. This now had to be faced with a thin skin of Das modelling clay, and the scribing needed to be the same as the bridge abutments, thereby creating an extensive slate wall that curved from both sides to connect with the railway bridge abutments.

The elevated section to the right is supported on a high stone embankment wall. The walling was made using cereal packet cardboard, which bends easily to follow the curvature required. This was then covered in a skin of Das, and scribed to represent stone masonry. The supporting buttress was made up from the same materials.

To finish the walls I added low parapet walls topped with upright coping stones. These were simply constructed from small 6 x 6mm balsa blocks, cutting it into short lengths of around 12mm. These were placed along the top edge of the embankment wall and glued into position, butting them up to each other. Once the low wall was complete, Das was again added, blending it into the main face of the embankment walling. To top this parapet the copings were made first, by rolling a sausage of Das and securing this with PVA to the top edge. The Das was smeared on the sides to blend it with the blocks; this can be executed by simply wetting your fingers first.

Once the whole construction and the Das had completely dried out, it needed to be scribed following the pattern of the slate masonry of the rest of the walling; however, the coping stones had to be scribed in a vertical pattern. To finish the walls, try chopping in with the scalpel or hobby knife to give a more authentic result to this type of coping.

Painting followed, referring to photographs in order to replicate the shades of the slate. This was achieved using the same mixes of artist's oil paint used on the previous sections of walling and the two stone bridges.

This now completes the making of the stone embankment walls; the weathering effects would be added later using dry-brushing techniques.

THE FRONT OF THE DIORAMA

CONSTRUCTING THE CLIFFS

With the embankment walls almost finished, the cliffs at the front of the diorama could be addressed. These would be constructed in two parts, beginning with the rock faces rising from the river. Construction started using blocks of polystyrene packaging, which was roughly carved using a bread knife. Careful carving gave a reasonable replication of the strata.

The completed waterfall can clearly be seen. The rocks at the base of the two packhorse bridges are built up from cork bark.

Cork bark gives a good replication of the rock face.

However, I mixed the polystyrene with cork bark, as the combination of both materials gave a more realistic result. The natural texture of the bark surface was ideal, with no extra carving required.

Cork bark is now readily available from model suppliers. I used the packs from Javis 'Countryside' Scenics range, although you need to be selective and choose pieces that will suit your requirements. I still used blocks of polystyrene to create the backing for the cork to be glued to, creating the face. The cork can be sawn, or in some cases broken, giving a more irregular and natural-looking edge when joining two pieces together. It is always worth playing around with pieces to see how they fit with each other. When you are happy, the pieces of cork can be secured to the polystyrene using PVA glue. Any large, unsightly gaps can be filled using Das modelling clay, which can be sculpted to blend to match the facing texture of the bark.

Assembly can be quite demanding, but with careful selection and positioning, you should be rewarded with realistic results. If in doubt, go and look at real cliff faces to see how the rock appears, and how the forces of nature have shaped them. This also applies to the painted finish, of course, which will be the next stage to consider.

Painting Cork and Polystyrene

Painting the cork with oil paint should not throw up any problems; however, it would not be advisable to use this medium when painting any of the carved polystyrene. The turpentine used to thin down the paint will instantly react with this material and dissolve it. To avoid this happening use a water-based medium – acrylic paint is ideal. In most cases I would never recommend the use of turpentine and oil paint with polystyrene, but there are exceptions to this. The effects of the dissolving can look realistic, especially in the lower rock faces where the river water has eaten into it over time. I used this technique at the river level on 'Raven's Ravine' and was pleased with the result, but careful attention must be observed as you could end up with the polystyrene being completely eaten away.

Moving on, the second part of the construction consists of a number of steps leading to the higher medieval arched bridge, the pathway to the lower bridge, and the caves that feature on the right-hand corner of the diorama.

CONSTRUCTING THE STEPS

3mm foam board was selected to build up the flight of steps. The method requires using strips of the 3mm foam board cut to about 1in (25mm) wide, starting with a strip cut to the longest length. This

Looking at the diorama from a distance: in the construction so far, on the right-hand side the embankment is complete, including the balsa-wood strips making up the backing supports. In front of this, the cliffside above the river has been built up using polystyrene packaging, roughly sawn to shape using the bread knife. The bridges are now complete, apart from the steps leading to the higher packhorse bridge. In the background the high ground has been started using blocks of insulation foam.

More or less the same view, although in the centre of the image the steps have been added; these have been constructed by overlapping strips of 3mm foam board.

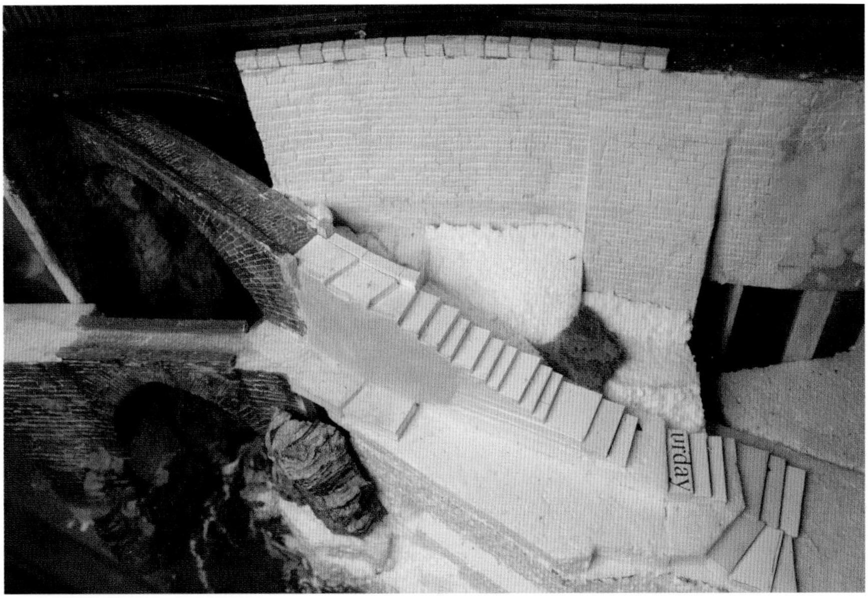

In this view looking down, it can be seen that some of the steps are much wider than others. Blocks of balsa wood have been attached to the top of the embankment wall.

A closer view of the ravine and the three bridges: all the masonry has now been scribed on the steps, before being painted to match in with the bridge.

would form the bottom step, and then a series would be cut with the next strip being slightly shorter than the previous strip, thus creating the rising steps. These would rise from the level to link up with the abutment to the bridge. Most would be positioned equally spaced out, with the tread being about 6mm wide; however, a few were made much wider. These would appear at the bottom of the flight, and one near to the bottom of the flight. This was purposely positioned so a special figure could be included, standing on this wider step.

Once this flight of steps was complete, facing texture could be applied to both the step treads and risers, and the face to this series of stone steps. To create the texture I used 'No More Cracks' plaster filler applied with a medium filbert brush to both the risers and the tread of each step. For the facing wall of the steps Das was used again, in the same way as was carried out on the stone embankment. The Das needed to be scribed when dry to match the masonry on the stone embankment and to link with the masonry of the medieval bridge.

CONSTRUCTING THE PATHWAY

The next challenge was to carry the pathway on round a hairpin bend to continue across the front and top of the cliffs rising from the river to reach the lower bridge. This was mainly constructed from mount card, and a few low steps were added, dropping to the deck level of this bridge. Once this had been fixed in position, a thin coat of Das was applied to the face, and a little to blend the sides to the rocky terrain. When dry the Das was scribed, though this time a rough pattern was attempted, to replicate irregular cobbles.

All could now be painted in exactly the same way as described previously with painting the embankment walling and the two stone bridges.

CONSTRUCTING THE ROCK TERRAIN AND CAVES

The rock terrain filling the corner of this diorama was to feature a series of caves. The first section to tackle was situated behind the bottom of the flight of steps. For this I selected pieces of cork bark that fitted nicely into the space. A slit was gouged through the cork using a knife and a woodworking chisel, creating a slender entrance for the first cave.

The rock terrain filling the corner was made using a chunk of insulation foam. This was first roughly cut to shape using a saw, and was then cut away at the rear to create a recess, which would form the inside of the caves. This was positioned and checked a number of times, and any excess foam cut away until it blended with the cork, fitting into the corner position neatly. The entrances to three caves were then cut into the front face. More sculpting was carried out both on the rock face and into the entrances, with the centre cave slightly larger than the outer two.

With this piece now sculpted, it could be fixed into position and glued. Any annoying joins would need to be filled with plaster and Das, to make them look more natural. The insulation foam still needed to be textured, to give a more authentic finish to the rock surface. I found that a coat of 'No More Cracks' plaster mix, together with PVA, gave the finish I was looking for.

Filling in the ground area behind the series of steps. Chunks of cork bark have again been used to form the rocks, together with polystyrene for the landform.

More prototype inspiration was found in Derbyshire at 'Hermit's Cave', ideal for the dragon's cave on the model.

A general view of the ravine, showing the landform in the centre now coated with plaster, and the dragon's cave to the right, carved out from insulation foam.

The dragon's cave and the landforms around it, painted using washes of oil paint.

Looking down on the central area of the model. The steps are now complete, along with the dragon's cave. Scenic scrub including ivy has been added above the cave and up to the embankment walling. All the rock faces below the pathway have been added, using a combination of cork bark and plaster, and painted using washes of oil paint.

Both sections making up this rocky terrain needed to be joined to the high stone walling supporting the railway above. This required landscaping with a grassy bank, punctuated with some exposed rocky outcrops. First a light support was made up using strips of card, then strips of plaster bandage were added to create the landform. Small chunks of cork bark were used to form the outcrops of rock; these were positioned with the plaster bandage running up to them. More plaster was brushed on to the surface of the plaster bandage, and then carefully brushed in around the exposed rocks.

Applying Surface Texture

To finish, this small area would need to be grassed over using static grass fibres. I always paint in the ground colour first, made up from mixing yellow ochre with Payne's grey. For static grass I selected the short fibres supplied by 'Greenscene', as I find these are perfect in length and colour. Remember we are trying to recreate wild grass, so don't be tempted to use just one colour of green. Always look towards using a few fibres of different shades of green, and try adding some straw-coloured fibres as well. This colour will represent the dead grass or dry grass found in the summer months.

Another tip when selecting static grass fibres is to pick out the more subdued green shades rather than the brighter green shades. The reason for this is that we are creating a miniature world, and everything will be scaled down, including colour.

The grassy bank will also require a few shrubs and undergrowth to create a wilder appearance. For this, a mixture of scenic materials such as foam flock and natural lichens can be used. I also included a few creepers clinging to the high embankment wall – there are now good representations of ivy and other creepers from Mini Natur, and the foliage matting from 'Woodland Scenics' always works well when teased out to length.

Moving back to the rock terrain and caves: these are now surface textured, but they still require painting and weathering to finish. For reference, I studied photographs of the gritstone and sandstone rock formations found at Hawkstone Park in Shropshire.

Artist's oil paint was again used for the sandstone colour of the caves, mixing and applying the darker shades first, then the lighter shades; this was followed by adding the highlights and weathering. The darker shades were created by mixing Payne's grey with yellow ochre, and the lighter colours by mixing burnt umber, yellow ochre and a little Naples yellow. The mix was applied using a stippling technique, with the paint nearly dry.

CREATING THE UPPER LANDFORM AND ROCK STRATA

Next to tackle are the upper levels of this model diorama, which will all appear above the track bed of the railway. The whole concept of this diorama would see it divided in two by the deep ravine. Therefore, two separate upper landforms would be required, one to the left and one to the right. The right-hand side was tackled first, using a chunk of insulation foam cut roughly to size. This was positioned temporarily, first to give an idea of the depth, and second to see what further carving was required to create the contours. I purposely cut the facing side back enough to include the steep, angled rock strata that would eventually be a major feature on this side of the diorama. This side would also include a rock tunnel, so the insulation foam was cut back from the track bed to accommodate this. The tunnel would be made up from a combination of layers of insulation foam and broken up pieces of insulation board.

Another consideration when cutting the main block was to cut away a recess on the ravine side. This was to allow for the positioning of the largest round castle tower, as this would need to appear as if it were rising up from the sheer rock face. I used an old bread-knife blade for all the cutting back and the final carving of the contours; I also used fine sandpaper on the contours. The block of insulation foam could now be glued into position, set back from the track bed.

THE FIRST CASTLE TOWER

The next task was to build up the rocks at the top of the ravine. This would include the first castle tower, which would appear at the front of the ravine. With this tower rising from the rock face, the bottom section would need to be addressed. This part of the tower was made from a gravy granules cardboard carton, which was ideal for this purpose as the diameter was just right; it also had a card rim that would form an architectural string course feature.

The modelled volcanic rocks, folded to a 40-degree angle, made from insulation board coated with 'No More Cracks' ready-mixed plaster: this created the surface texture. They are positioned to surround the base section of the castle tower, which is made from a cardboard gravy carton.

The bottom part of this tower would be partly hidden by the rock formation, but some of the lower tower would be exposed, so the masonry would need to be included. Before this, a window aperture was cut into the side of the carton, with a stone mullion frame cut out of mounting card and fixed into position. Das modelling clay was pushed on to the outside of the carton, using the fingers. Once the clay had completely dried out, the rubble stone masonry was then scribed out in the usual way. With this done, the tower was glued into position.

CREATING THE ROCK STRATA

With this part of the tower now complete apart from painting and weathering, I could start to surround part of the structure with the rock strata. I selected chunks of insulation foam, carving them to shape. I used reference photographs, again taken at Hawkstone Park where many interesting formations can be found that were ideal to try to replicate for this model. The carved rocks were positioned and glued together, some standing upright against the castle tower. When gluing the rocks together, I also used cocktail sticks to give extra support on the joins. Some of the more awkward gaps were filled with Das modelling clay.

The next stage was to give all the carved rocks a surface texture, which was achieved by coating them with a mix of PVA with 'No More Cracks' plaster filler. This always gives a realistic finish, especially for rocks, as well as a good number of masonry textures. Once this was dry, the painting stage could be addressed. Once again oil paint was used, adding the darker shades first, then building up the lighter shades, using both stippling and dry-brushing techniques.

When it comes to painting and weathering the rock formations, always refer to photographs. These will be challenging, as they will consist of many shades of colour when you include the weathering and lichen growth on the surface. One technique that can be used to replicate the latter is to flick on the paint from an old toothbrush. For this technique the colours will need to be mixed first, then thinned down with a good amount of turpentine. The paint is then applied to the toothbrush, and by flicking the bristles of the brush towards the rock the paint is finely splattered over the surface to give a very realistic effect. This technique can also be used to create lichen growth on other items, including tree bark.

INSPIRATION FOR DRAMATIC VOLCANIC ROCK FORMATIONS

Moving on, the next section of this upper level will require the modelling of more rock formations. This time, however, the rock strata will differ to that reproduced in the immediate area of the ravine. I wanted to try and include rock formations that had originally been laid down in horizontal layers. Some

The volcanic lava rock formations found at Beacon Hill, Leicestershire.

Inspiration came from the volcanic rocks rising from Beacon Hill.

More extreme terrain, with dramatic rock panicles. These limestone crags are Harborough Rocks, deep in the White Peak District of Derbyshire.

The extreme rocky terrain known as The Stiperstones, an exposed ridge in west Shropshire.

600 million years ago, during the Pre-Cambrian period, the violent geological forces of the earth pushed and pulled the horizontal rock layers to form steep angles, causing these rocks to jut up out of the ground in spectacular formations.

Before trying to model this, I needed to take a look at prototypes where this action could be seen for real. I had already done some research on the internet and found a location not too far away from home. This was at Beacon Hill in the Charnwood Forest area of Leicestershire, the highest part of the west of the county, and well known for the exposed rock formations found there. The rocks are some of the oldest to be found in England and Wales, formed 600 million years ago during the Pre-Cambrian period from volcanic ash that settled and solidified on what was then a seabed. Volcanic rocks are very hard and resistant to erosion by the elements, which is why they constitute the dramatic rocky outcrops we see dominating the highest ground of the area today.

MODELLING VOLCANIC ROCK

The next thing to consider was finding materials that would replicate this type of rock. After looking at the materials available I settled on fibre board, which was used extensively in the building trade for wall insulation. Today this material has been superseded by insulation foam for this use. However, it can still be found, and a thinner version is now used as a foundation for laminate flooring.

One reason for choosing this material was its composition. The board is made up of multiple layers of fibres bonded tightly together, the main advantage of this material being that it can be easily broken by hand. This creates a realistic finish, replicating the layering of this type of rock, as well as shales such as slate. Pieces of fibre board can be glued together and piled up to create layered rock formations.

This was used on the diorama to make up the rock formations facing and topping the right-hand raised landform. I wanted to create the rock strata rising from the ground at conflicting angles. This would look more dramatic than just laying them down flat. Looking at prototypes I found many samples where the movement of the earth had pushed and folded the rock strata, resulting in steep angles formed and some even appearing nearly vertical. After my visit I found evidence of this action taking place at Beacon Hill, so I was able to use my reference photographs taken on site.

To create the angles required, the first task was to include a supporting block inserted under one end of the first layer of insulation board, with the broken edge facing outwards. This could then be adjusted until the desired angle was achieved. Once satisfied with the result, then a second piece could be placed on top, again with the broken edge facing outwards. This would be followed by a third piece, and so on, all securely glued together using a thick coat of PVA.

I decided to feature two large rocks jutting out at an angle; this would set off the castle tower perfectly. All the other rock formations were set to the opposite angle to the first one, to create a fold in the strata. This formation of strata would make up the rock cutting and the rock tunnel that featured on the right-hand side of the model.

The whole of the modelled rocky volcanic terrain dominating the upper right-hand side of the diorama.

The steep-angled volcanic rock formations can be seen in this photograph at Beacon Hill.

More dramatic rock formations at Beacon Hill: there is plenty of reference for modelling extreme terrain.

The broken edge of the insulation board. Note how the fibrous core provides a good replication of shale strata.

More modelled rock strata forming the rock tunnel. Note how the strata are folded in the opposite direction.

The coming together of the modelled rock strata.

Another view of the rock strata that forms the cave-like tunnel.

In this view of the tunnel the small rock panicles can be seen formed above.

The rocks would still require a facing texture, which was achieved in the same way as the sandstone and gritstone by using a coat of 'No More Cracks' plaster mix. Painting, however, would require matching the paint shades to this type of stone. This is where it is important to take close-up photographs as reference for colour matching. Close examination will reveal rich variations of browns, greens and greys: these will be represented in oil paint, which will need careful mixing and application; this will also include the final finish and weathering. (This is covered in more detail in the colour guide at the back of this book.)

Moving on to the higher part of the landform, all the hillside would need grassing over. This was achieved by using static grass applied over a dark painted ground colour, as used previously. The area would also include a ring of standing stones, as well as loose stone scree and more outcrops of rock punctuating the upper part of this hill.

STANDING STONES, SCREE AND OUTCROPS

I used natural slate chippings and flakes for the standing stones, the slate outcrops and the broken loose scree. The natural slate was obtained from Natural

The ancient standing stones on Harthill Moor, Derbyshire, gave me the inspiration for a similar group of standing stones to feature in the model.

The standing stones on the model were made using flakes of real slate, available from Natural Scenics.

Scenics, who supply packs of graded slate, which was perfect for use on this diorama.

The stone circle was constructed using selected larger chippings of the slate, picking them out for shape. I used reference photographs taken at Harthill Moor in Derbyshire, although these consisted of gritstone rather than slate; however, they were very helpful when picking out individual shapes to use for the slate. The position of the standing stones would be on the flatter part of the land in the central area.

Once selected, the larger chips of slate were positioned, with five of them planted and pushed into the soft insulation foam and secured with glue to make up a circle. I purposely planted two at a slight angle, with the others totally upright. The reference photographs also helped with this decision.

THE FOLLY

MAKING THE SITE FOR THE FOLLY

I planned to situate the folly in the rear right-hand corner of the raised land. It needed to be on slightly higher ground to the standing stones, therefore extra height was built up using pieces of insulation board roughly cut to shape with a craft knife, and glued into position. I already had a plan of the folly, so the footprint could be marked on the top of the insulation board. I then added some plaster bandage to create a gradually sloping bank to the facing edges. This was all painted in the ground colour, before adding more short fibres of static grass, but leaving the footprint clear.

The next task was to add the exposed outcrops of rock to this area. For these I used chunks of broken insulation board, together with some larger chips of natural slate. The pieces of insulation board required both texturing and painting in the same way, but the slate could remain the natural colour.

Once the upright rocks had been secured and finished, the loose rock scree was added, selecting the larger chippings first, then decreasing in size to the smaller flakes of slate. This was spread out to represent scree falling away from the exposed rocky outcrops. Reference photographs were used again for all the stages, to gain a good understanding of how this should appear in miniature on the model.

POSITIONING THE FOLLY

I had originally intended for the folly to be positioned in the foreground alongside the castle tower, but then there would have been too many structures appearing together. By using a cut-down cardboard tube as a mock-up and moving this around, it soon became apparent that the folly would look much better positioned right at the back of the hill on the highest ground. The making or using of a rough mock-up is always worth considering when you are not sure where to position a structure or building on your layout or diorama.

At this time, I also decided to scale down the folly in size slightly. All the structures appearing in the foreground – or for that matter the mid-ground – would be modelled at 4mm scale, but the folly was going to stand right at the back and in the far corner on the highest point, so it could therefore appear smaller. By modelling it in 3mm scale rather than 4mm, it would look correct according to the laws of perspective.

PROTOTYPES FOR THE FOLLY

For this folly I could have made something up using my imagination. A folly however, would be built with no practical use other than a whimsical structure to enhance a viewpoint in the landscape. This means that there are a few prototypes that would suit my requirement for the diorama. I ended up looking at two possibilities, these being 'Mow Cop' in Cheshire or 'Old John' standing in Bradgate Park near to Leicester. In the end I decided to choose the latter as this would fit the space available.

With the choice now made, the next stage was to visit the site at Bradgate Park to photograph 'Old John' and where possible take actual measurements, and if not, some estimated measurements. Along with these, more general photographs were taken of the folly, with a good number of close-ups as well. Close-ups always come in handy, especially for the final painting and weathering of a structure. When making a site visit it is advisable to take with you a camera, and of course a tape measure, also a sight-

'Old John', the folly that dominates the landscape of 'Bradgate Park' in west Leicestershire. This folly was chosen as a prototype as it would make a visually interesting feature to add to the rear of the diorama.

The tube was covered with a skin of Das modelling clay, with all the rubble stone and brick lintels scribed out.

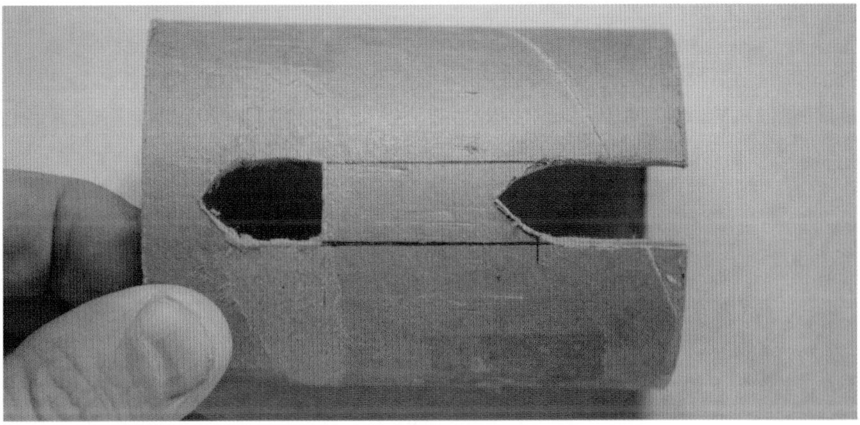

The starting point for modelling the folly was a cardboard parcel tube. The Gothic-topped window and door have first been marked and then cut out.

ing pole to use when estimating heights, and lastly a notepad and pen to record all this information.

CONSTRUCTING THE FOLLY

With the information now to hand, I could draw up a scale drawing. The folly mainly consisted of the round castle tower, which would be the starting point for the model. Using the drawing, I searched for a cardboard postal tube that was as near to the diameter as possible. Once found, the next task was to cut the tube with a saw to a length representing the height of the folly. This was followed by cutting through the tube to create the window and door apertures. In real life the folly was built from local stone, so a skin of Das modelling clay was applied to the tube's surface, followed by scribing the rubble stone and brick lintels.

CREATING THE CASTLE TOWER CRENELLATIONS

The castle tower was topped with crenellations, which were slightly wider than the tower itself. With my desire to reuse packaging I found a mustard jar lid that was just the right diameter. (Always be on the lookout for packaging that might come in useful for your model-making needs.) To create the crenellations a strip of thin card was cut to the depth required, and the crenellations were first marked out to size and then cut out. The thin card was easy to bend around the outside rim of the jar top, and was then glued to it. The card was far too thin, and needed to be backed with thicker card to create the depth of the crenellations. These were cut to size and glued into position with a separate block of card for each.

Creating the crenellations at the top of the tower started with the lid of a mustard jar.

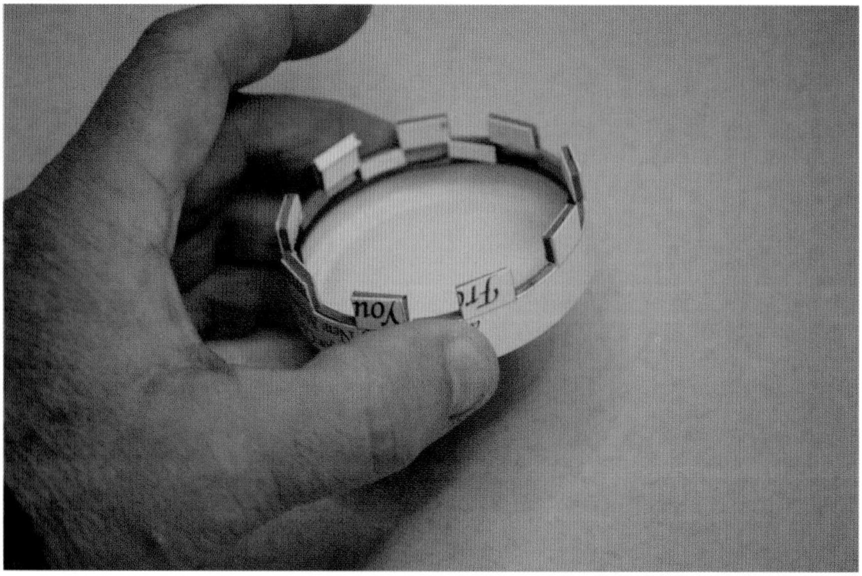

The crenellations were cut from thin greetings card and backed up with thicker card. The thinner card was wrapped around the jar lid and fixed to it, and then the backing was added.

The crenellations now needed topping out with pitched stone copings. For these, I used the angled styrene strip supplied by Evergreen, selecting the 2mm width. These were cut slightly over length for the high crenellations, and exactly to length for the lower ones, and were glued on using superglue. This almost completed the top of the tower.

The final process was the texturing required to give the entire top a stone finish. This was achieved by painting on a mix of PVA and 'No More Cracks' ready-mixed plaster. At this time any awkward gaps appearing at the back between the thicker card blocks were also filled in using the same plaster mix.

The top could now be brought together with the main round tower, and superglued into position. To complete the join a 1.5mm thick card strip was cut to about 3mm wide. This was then wrapped around to mask the join, and also to create the string coursing of stone as seen on the prototype.

PAINTING THE MASONRY

Before fitting the windows and the door, it is best to paint all the masonry. The mortar used on the tower was almost white, so this colour was used first as a wash and brushed all over. This only takes about twenty minutes to dry, so the greyish-brown colour for the stone was then mixed and dry brushed over, with some areas appearing darker than others, replicating the prototype as closely as possible. A reddish-brown shade was mixed for the small amount of brickwork visible over the window and door. I applied the weathering later, when the joining arch had been attached to the tower.

FITTING THE WINDOWS AND THE DOOR

Once the masonry paintwork had completely dried, the window and door could be fitted. The tower did have two more windows, but because these were at the rear, and the tower was positioned right at the back of the diorama, they would not be seen. Both the window and the door frame have to fit inside the pre-cut aperture, following the shape including the Gothic top. I first traced the shape of the aperture on to a piece of tracing paper, and then transferred this to the inside of an old greetings card. I then drew the inside of the window frame, which was about 1.5mm wide and included the Gothic shapes at the top of the frame. The bottom two-thirds had wooden shutters fitted, so this was left as a solid panel.

Once satisfied with the drawing, it was then very carefully cut out. Before this was done, however, a strip of double-sided tape was applied to the rear of the card. This was done to attach the clear film to the top section, creating the glazing. The window frame could now be married up with the aperture and carefully secured with glue.

The door was produced in the same way, although for this the inside of the frame was not required. The vertical planking of the door was scribed on before fitting. Do this with the point of a knife blade, drawing it back towards you against the edge of a steel rule. This will make a 'V' groove in the surface of the card, giving a good impression of vertical boarding.

To finish, the frames and door were painted a mid-brown colour, following the prototype.

THE GOTHIC ARCH

Next to address was the Gothic arch, which adjoined the round tower on one side. Looking at my reference drawing, the profile was transferred by making a tracing on to a piece of 6mm foam board. This was

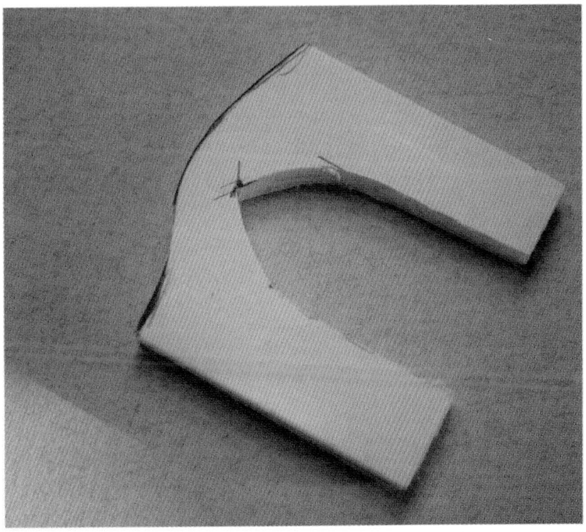

The adjoining wall with its large Gothic arch has been marked and then cut out from 6mm foam board.

The folly is now nearly complete: the adjoining wall has now been fixed to the main round tower, all the masonry has been painted by dry brushing, the top window with its shutters has been fitted, and the coping stones that top each of the crenellations have been fixed in place.

then glued to another piece of 6mm foam board, making it double thickness. The rugged outline was now cut out, cutting through the 12mm thickness of the board, leaving straight the one side where the extension would be joined to the main tower.

The archway could now be cut out, making sure that the two curves forming the top of the Gothic arch came together neatly. With the profile now cut out, Das clay was applied in the usual way, ready to scribe the rubble stone masonry. This matched the main round tower that was constructed of the same rubble stone. The top edge was chopped into to emulate the ruined broken edge. This was intentionally built into the prototype, as most follies were purposely built to represent a sham ruin.

The added-on wall with the Gothic archway needed painting in the same way as the tower; when completely dry it could be married up with the tower to finish the folly of 'Old John'.

FIXING THE FOLLY IN POSITION

The finished folly could now be fixed into position, dominating the top of the high land. The sizing down of this structure worked well, making it look further away when viewed from the front of the diorama. I added some fine flock at the base, so it blended in perfectly with the surrounding landscape as well as masking the joining gaps.

The finished folly located on the model, fitting in nicely with the surrounding landscape.

FINISHING THE CASTLE TOWER

The right-hand side of the upper landform was now complete, but I had not finished the castle tower, so this now needed to be addressed. For the next section a cardboard postal tube was selected. Unfortunately I could not find one of the correct diameter, so to solve this problem I added some corrugated cardboard wrapped around the tube, which made up the difference. This was fitted to the previous round base carton and secured – though before this was done, the masonry was added using a skin of Das modelling clay.

The top section could now be tackled, and for this a postal tube was found of the correct diameter, this being slightly less than the middle section. The top edge of this was chopped away, giving the ruin its rugged appearance. This section would also require an arrow loop to be positioned about half way up. This was duly cut through the tube, replicating a cross; it was cleaned up on the sides before Das was added. The clay was taken over the rugged top edge, making up the thickness of this defensive tower.

All that remained was to paint the masonry and apply the final weathering. The same painting techniques were employed, using dry-brushed oil paint. This also included the weathering, where the rain staining was picked out forming dark streaks running down the stone masonry. To complete this tower and to add to the character of the ruin, I attached a few ivies growing and clinging to the stone walls. These were selected from the scenic range of 'Mini-Natur', and give a very convincing result.

UPPER GROUND FEATURES ON THE LEFT SIDE OF THE RAVINE

The upper ground features on the left-hand side of the ravine can now be addressed. The raised land was again started by selecting and cutting a slab of insulation foam, and this was shaped before the sandstone and gritstone rocks were added, rising from the track bed of the railway. These rocks were carved from the blocks of insulation foam to form rugged shapes replicating those already carved for the ravine. The rocks were textured and painted using the same techniques as before.

The upper part of this side of the diorama will also feature two more ruined castle towers, and these need to be modelled before the rocks can be finally placed because some of the rocks will surround the base of both towers. The two towers will be linked with sections of curtain walling, also in a ruined state, and these will also need to be fitted before the rocks.

My own illustration to show the ruins of Red Castle, taken from an early engraving of the main tower. This group of ruined towers provided the main inspiration for the ruins that front the diorama.

Another illustration taken from an early engraving, showing all three ruined towers. It also shows how they complement the rocky crags and caves of the dramatic landscape surrounding them. It was this type of dramatic setting I wanted to include in the diorama.

CONSTRUCTION OF THE TWO RUINED TOWERS

Both the ruined towers will be built using scrap packaging in the same way as the first tower – the difference being that both these towers will feature a flared-out base. For the larger of the two towers I selected a card coffee cup to use for the base. The smaller tower's base was made up with a polystyrene tub, the sort used by the local fish and chip shop to carry gravy or mushy peas in.

Moving on to the next section of both towers, I used two cardboard toilet roll centres, one slightly wider than the other: the wider one fitted on top of the card coffee cup, and the one with the smaller diameter fitted perfectly on the polystyrene tub. This just left the two top sections to be sorted out. On the first tower modelled, positioned on the right-hand

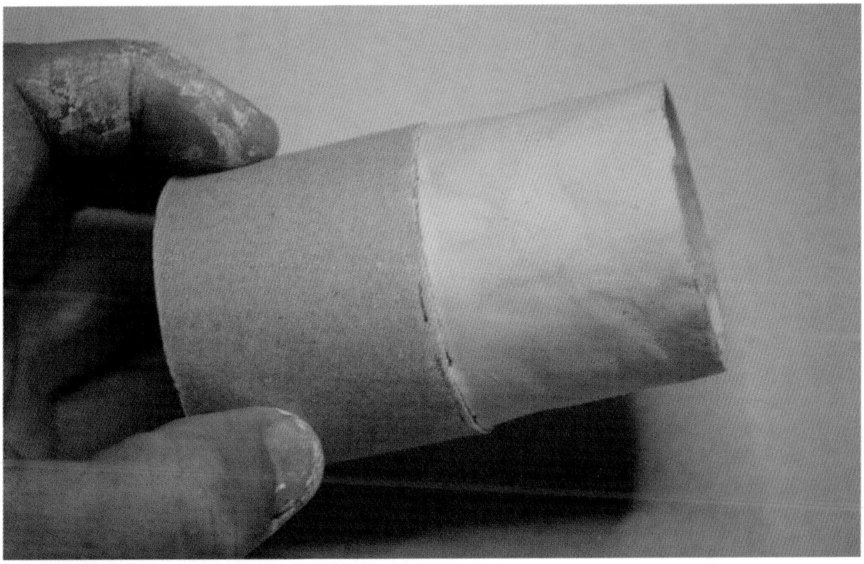

The first stage in the construction of the towers, using cardboard packaging and postal tubes, which have been brought together and telescoped to form the basis of the towers.

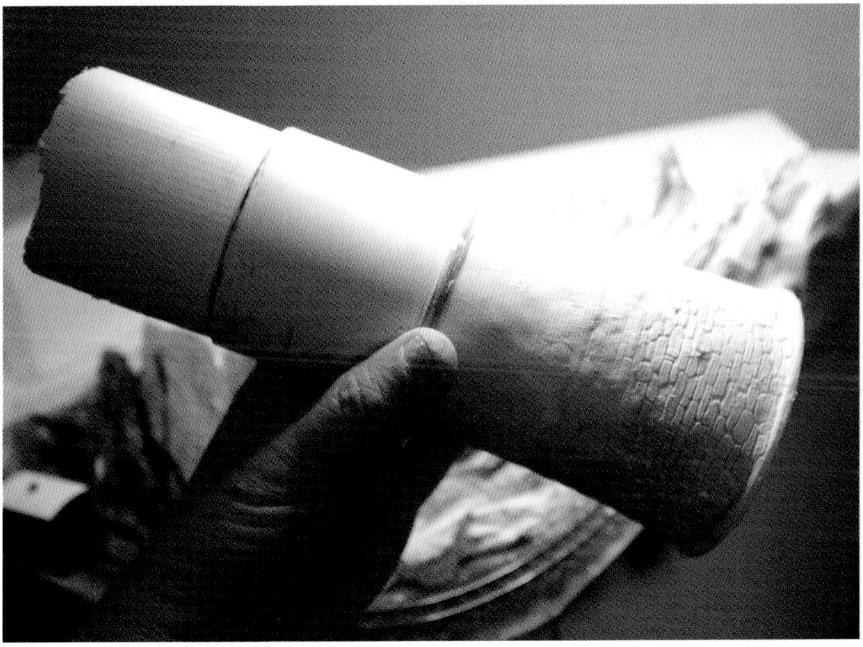

Two tubes telescoped together, the flared base made from a card drinks carton.

General view of the whole diorama with the three towers temporarily placed in position to see how they will look.

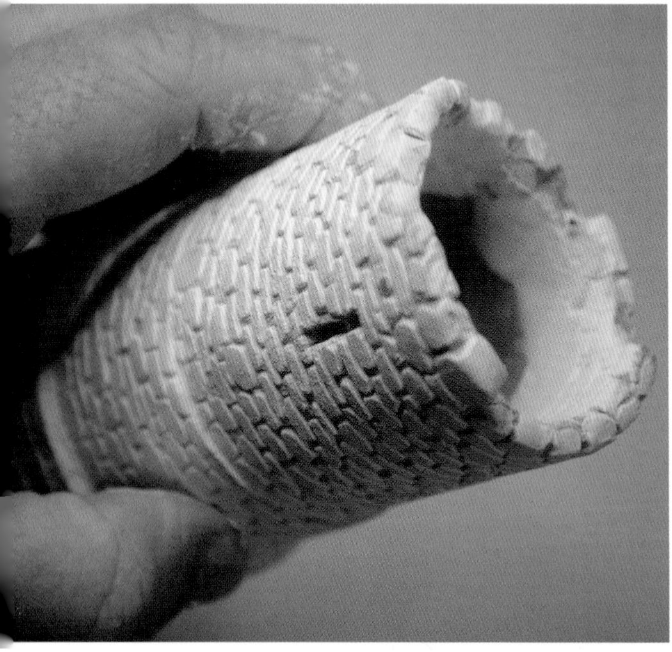

The top of the tower already skinned with Das and all scribed out; also note the arrow slit has been cut out. The broken top edge to the tower is produced by adding extra clay to the inside, then chopping away to represent the ruined top.

The prototype reference for the ruined masonry and colour tones came from the ruins of Codnor Castle.

The second tower, all scribed with rubble stone masonry ready for painting. The top section is made from a postal tube, followed by two toilet roll centres of different diameter, and the flared base from a drinks carton.

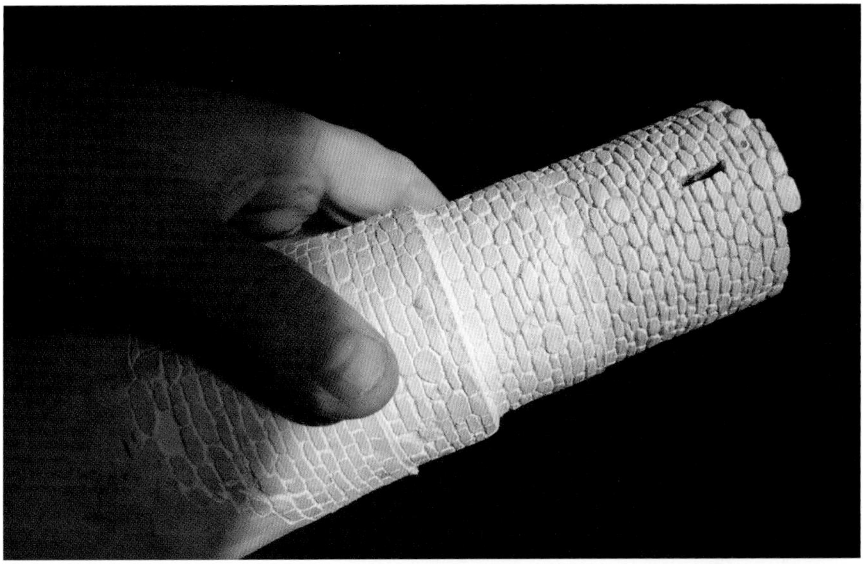

side of the ravine, a thick postal tube was selected. I decided that this would be the best solution for the two smaller towers, although the tubes selected needed to be smaller in diameter.

In both of the top sections arrow slits needed to be cut out, and the irregular, broken masonry carved to replicate the ruined state of the towers. When cutting and carving the thicker card of the postal tubes, extreme care must be taken.

The next step was to add Das modelling clay to all three sections before they were assembled together. The clay will adhere to the card of the coffee cup and the polystyrene of the tub, although a good tip is to give them both a liberal coat of PVA first.

The clay will adhere to the card of the toilet roll centres and the postal tubes with no problem. Once the clay has completely dried, the rubble stone masonry can be scribed out in the usual way.

With the two towers now scribed out, the sections can be glued together. If an awkward gap is visible on any of the joins, then this can be easily rectified by smearing a little more Das into the join. The clay would need to be applied more thickly on the ruined top to create the thickness of the defensive walls.

The completed assembled towers can now be positioned but not glued, as the sections of curtain wall will need to be fitted in between.

The main tower is now complete, with all the painting and weathering finished. Note the window fitted in the lower section. Note also how the tower is embedded in the rock formation, looking as if it is growing out of the rocks. The ivy has also been replicated in miniature, clinging to the walls of this ruin.

The finished second tower, also embedded in the rocky terrain on the left side of the diorama.

CONSTRUCTION OF THE RUINED CURTAIN WALLS

Before constructing the walls, the gap between the two towers will need to be measured out, along with the profile of the flared bases, so this steep angle can be transferred to the walls. The material chosen for the curtain wall sections was 6mm foam board. I glued two pieces together face to face, to give the thickness required.

The curtain walls needed to be of a reasonable thickness, making them as unbreakable as possible. Once the profile to each side had been plotted on both sections, an irregular line was drawn on the top, to represent the broken, ruined masonry, matching the towers. To make the top look more realistic, the outer 6mm foam board was cut slightly larger on the inner board. This helps to create that rugged appearance, especially when the clay has been added and carved.

With the wall sections now cut out, they can be covered with a skin of Das modelling clay: this was applied fairly thickly and taken over the top and on to the inside. Once the clay had dried, the rubble stone masonry could be scribed, with the stone carved and even chopped into, so as to create the rugged, broken top.

The next task was to join up the sections of curtain wall with the castle towers. Once happy with the positioning, both the towers and the walling sections could be glued and secured. Although the profile had been cut as accurately as possible, there was a slight gap visible. This was soon remedied using a little more clay as filler.

All that was needed now was to paint all the masonry using the media and methods already described.

THE SECOND TUNNEL

While tackling the curtain walls it was logical to address the second tunnel, which would take the narrow-gauge railway under the abbey ruins. These ruins were planned so as to create the focal point on the highest part of the diorama. The raised land was constructed using more of the foam board – this would extend from the main block of insulation foam on this side of the diorama. The extension was completely made of foam board and needed to cover the railway.

A top was cut out, and was supported by a section of board on the far edge. Extra supporting panels were also added at the front and the rear. A gap was left at the front for the railway to run through. This gap would be filled with a stone-arched tunnel mouth, set forward by about 40mm. This would allow for the land above to slope down slightly from the highest level. I liked the idea of the tunnel mouth linking with the curtain walling, and this could be easily achieved by constructing a wing wall on the right-hand side.

The tunnel mouth itself was marked out, making sure there was enough clearance for the rolling stock to clear the walls on the steep curve. Once this had been achieved, the vertical sides were drawn out, along with an arch that was added to the top. I used a tin lid as a template to draw this out before cutting out the semi-circular archway.

The raised landform on the left was extended to accommodate the tunnel, and the base for the ruins of the abbey.

This photograph shows how the abbey ruins will fit over the tunnel.

The tunnel entrance, cut out from 6mm foam board, and temporarily positioned to make sure it fitted with the surrounding landform on the right-hand side.

The tunnel mouth now coated with Das, with all the stone masonry scribed out. The final stages of painting are in progress. A wing wall has been added up against the high landform on the right-hand side.

Once the foam board was all cut out, Das modelling clay was added, applying it a little thinner than the curtain walling. The tunnel mouth just needed painting, matching the rest of the stonework; this also needed a reasonable amount of weathering, especially the smoke staining produced by the steam trains going in and out of the tunnel.

The space between the edges of the main landform block and both the curtain walls and tunnel mouth could now be filled. A support was formed in the usual way, again with strips of card. These were glued at both ends, using pins until the glue had properly dried and the bond made. This was duly covered with plaster bandage to make a solid foundation for scenic material. Once dry and solid, this was painted a ground colour first, before static grass and flock were finally added.

FINISHING THE ROCKS

I could now go back to fixing the rocks, which were all carved from insulation foam and textured with 'No More Cracks' plaster filler. All the rocks were now glued into their final position, with a good number surrounding the base of the two ruined castle towers. It was important when positioning the rocks to make them look as natural as possible. I also left room to allow for an extension to be added on the pathway leading from the top packhorse bridge. This pathway would enter the catacombs of the castle through a Gothic arched door.

The pathway and arched doorway were made from card and coated with 'No More Cracks' to give added texture. All this was constructed and painted off set before being brought into position. More rock faces were made up on each side of the pathway once this and the arched door had finally been glued in. All the rocks could now be painted and weathered, which included replicating the lichen growth.

The rocks were painted by first applying a wash of oil paint in a dark colour made up by mixing raw umber with a little Payne's grey. The next stage was to apply the lighter shades to the rocks, using a stippling technique with a nearly dry mix of yellow ochre and titanium white paint. The same technique can also be used to add the lichen growth on the surface of the rock. Another painting technique used here was to flick the paint on to the surface of the rock from a toothbrush. This needs a little practice first, but the results can look very effective.

CONSTRUCTING THE ABBEY RUINS

These abbey ruins will be the diorama's focal point, standing on its highest part. Originally this area would have included more of the castle towers and associated buildings, but I decided that this would look too much, and that an alternative structure would be a better choice. Looking around for this alternative, I was inspired by some of the great abbey ruins to be found within the UK. It would not be practical to build too much of any one abbey's ruins, but would be better to pick out one part that would be visually appealing.

I planned a visit to Dale Abbey, which is local for me, standing between Derby and Ilkeston. There is not a great deal of it left today, as much of the stone has been reused for the construction of many build-

Illustration to show how the abbey ruins will hopefully appear on the model.

Prototype inspiration again, this time for the abbey ruins, which will feature over the tunnel. This is the large nave window, the only part of Dale Abbey left standing.

ings in the village. The end wall of the nave still stands proud, with its large Gothic window. The window lacks any of its lancets, and very little tracery remains, however, what did remain would be ideal to base this model on.

I wanted to add some extra features, and recreate some of the inside structure, although in a very ruined state. By looking through reference books and using my imagination I came up with a series of arches supported on stone columns. These would have once supported the upper walls of the nave, which had long since disappeared. Basically I wanted the ruins of the abbey to look romantic, and to give, in this three-dimensional model, the effect of one of those picturesque paintings of the past.

BUILDING THE NAVE END WALL

A start was made on the nave end wall by selecting two pieces of 6mm foam board. These were first cut to a basic size of 6 x 5in (152 x 128mm) and then glued together face to face.

The Arched Window

The arched window could now be plotted, first by measuring the centre line 2.5in (64mm) in from the edge. Next the width of the arch could be plotted and marked, by marking the vertical sides at 1.5in (38mm) away from the centre line. The height of both the sides and the top of the arch were now plotted, measured out at 3in (78mm) for the sides and 5in (127mm) for the top of the arch. To plot the large Gothic arch, a curve was needed: I used a circular template – a tea plate was ideal for this – with a diameter of 6in (152mm). Line up the edge of the plate with the two points where the height met both sides and joined up with the centre line.

With the arch now marked out, it can be cut out using a sharp blade in the scalpel or hobby knife: use a steel rule on the verticals, and the same tea plate to cut against for the curves. The top and right-hand side must now be cut away to make a broken edge. A good result can be achieved by cutting away the front foam board slightly in from the one at the rear. This will give a realistic stepped and broken rugged appearance to the right and top edges. Once the stepped edge has been cut, this could be worked on a little more by carving into the foam board.

The Upright Columns

The next task was to create some of the tracery on the inside edge of the Gothic arch. The sides were tackled first, by trying to recreate the upright columns made up on the original from separate carved blocks of stone. I found some wooden kebab skewers that were a reasonable diameter to replicate the stone columns. These were cut to length before securing the first section to the inside front of the side of the arch. The second column was glued to the side of the first, but slightly offset, with the third column glued on to the second, following the same pattern.

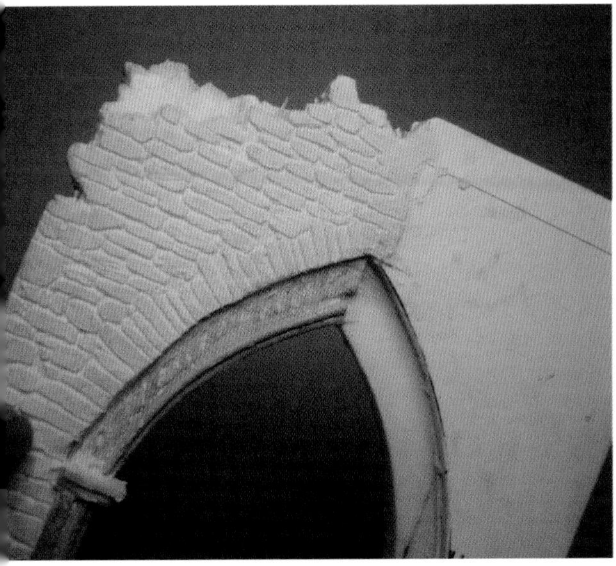

A similar window will feature on the abbey ruins for the model. In this view the end wall has been cut out from two pieces of 6mm foam board spliced together. The large Gothic arched window has been cut out, with the facing aperture cut out 8mm larger than the rear. This is to accommodate the decorative spandrels and columns. The left-hand side has been scribed, with the top edge chopped away to give a good impression of the ruin.

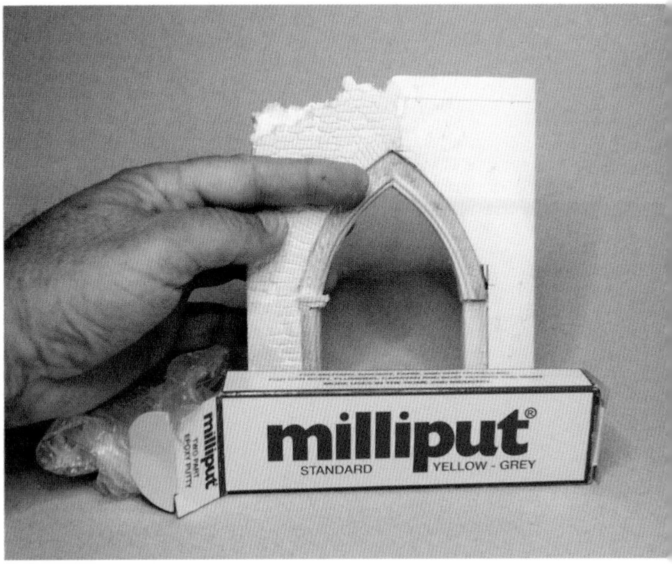

To form the decorative spandrels, styrene tube was used, curving it to follow the Gothic arch. Then Milliput was used to fill in the gap, with a scroll pattern embossed, using the rounded end of a coffee stirrer, before it had hardened.

The columns needed a backing to make them more secure, and this was easily remedied with a strip of card added to the rear of the foam board. The columns also required topping before moving on to the spandrels around the curvature of the arch. Both tops were cut, making two squares of 2mm mount card, with the top square overlapping the lower one by 2mm on three sides only. The tops were then glued into position, with the smaller square connected to the top of the columns. This was repeated on both sets of columns, making sure that they were both completely level.

The Inside Curvature of the Gothic Arch

The same rounded pattern of the vertical columns needed to be repeated on the inside curvature of the Gothic arch. This time, however, only two were required, though again one would slightly overlap the other. I could not use skewers as there was no way of bending them to follow the curve, and having looked at various materials that could easily be bent in this way, I settled on styrene hollow rod. By immersing the rod in boiling water for a while, the styrene became soft and easy to bend to shape. The styrene rod could now be glued into position and cut to fit, making sure that they came together neatly at the top point of the arch.

All gaps were filled using a filler such as Milliput, which was also used to fill and face the area between the styrene rod and the edge of the cut foam board. Before the filler hardened off, the end of a coffee stirrer was used to press in a repeated pattern, replicating some of the ornate tracery.

The Stone-Built Buttress

The nave end wall on the left side would feature a stone-built buttress. This was constructed from mounting board, with the side marked out with a 45-degree step halfway up, and again the same angle repeated at the top. Two sides were needed, then the

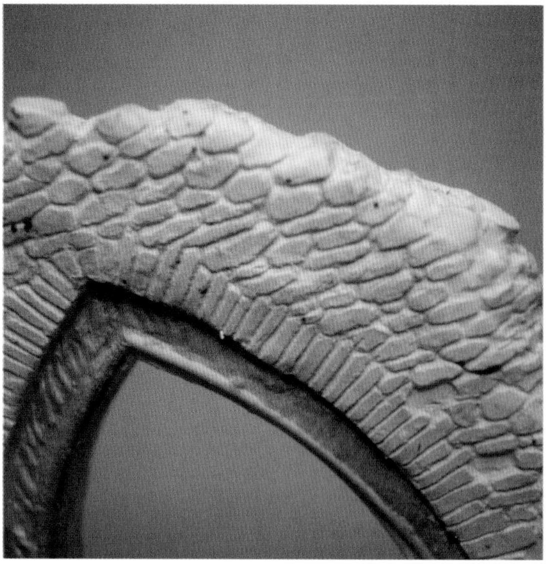

The finished scribing to the top edge replicating the ruined masonry. More Das has been added to create a realistic finish to the stonework that has broken away.

The end wall with two base feet added to hold the columns. Balsa wood was used to create these, with the facing edges carved and shaped.

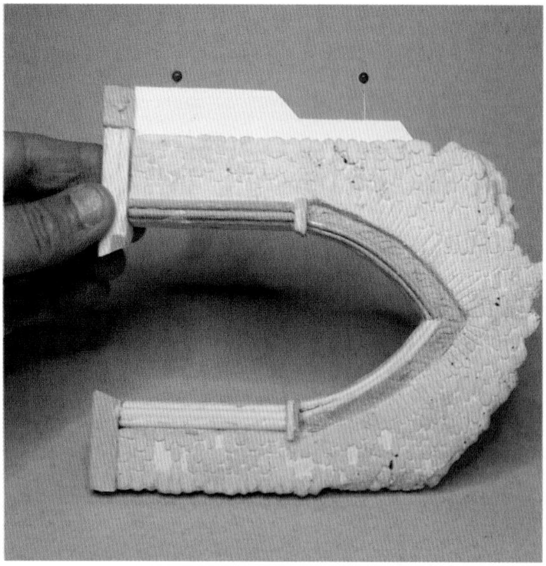

The buttress has been constructed from mounting card to support the end wall. Note also a further block of balsa wood has been fitted under the buttress.

The buttress covered with a skin of Das modelling clay.

The finished window end, with the buttress now scribed, and all the stonework painted and weathered to finish.

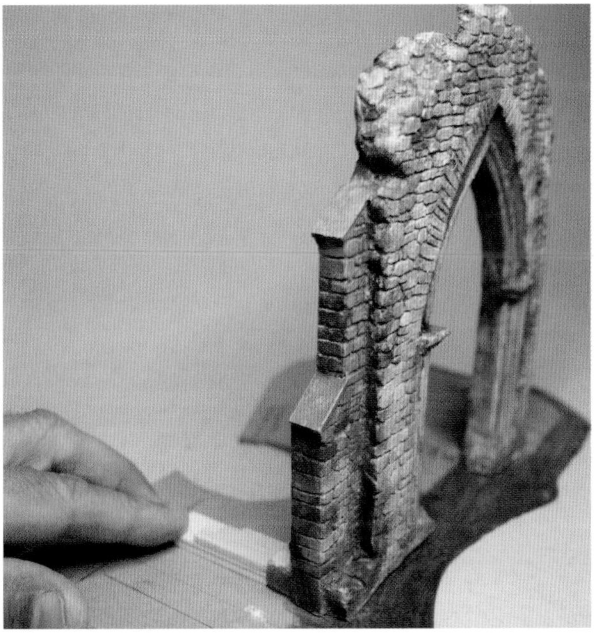

The window end from the three-quarter view. The paint finishes applied to the buttress can be seen clearly, along with the broken edge to the thick walls.

thickness of the buttress was made up from strips of balsa wood faced with card. Mounting board was used for the angled tops, cut to overlap slightly. I decided that the buttress and the bottom of the wall to the arch needed a base to sit on, and this was done using blocks of balsa wood cut square, measuring 15 x 15mm, and securing them in position with glue.

The construction was now complete, and all that there remained to do was to cover the whole end wall with a skin of Das modelling clay of around 2mm thick all over, including the broken edges. Once the clay had completely dried off, then the stone masonry could be scribed. Besides scribing the clay, it would need to be carved again on all the broken edges. This would add a realistic textured finish, to recreate an authentic-looking ruin.

CONSTRUCTION OF THE INSIDE ARCHES

Before moving on to the painting stage I needed to start the construction of the inside arches. These would be supported on a series of stone columns, which could have been made from scratch, but I found some 3D printed columns in the correct scale available from 'York Model Making'. These were ideal, and I purchased a set of four to use on this model.

I decided to make up the arches from foam board, first marking them out using a tin lid as a template. I only cut out one arch in full – the others were only part of the arch, which was to create the effect of the structure falling into ruin. All the foam-board arches were covered with a skin of Das modelling clay and then scribed out, while the tops were cut away to form a rugged irregular edge, giving the arches that romantic ruined appearance.

Overall view of the diorama to show the position of the abbey ruins in relation to the other structures.

The arches that would have supported the roof to the nave being cut from 3mm foam board. Tins and jar lids have been used as templates to help with the cutting out.

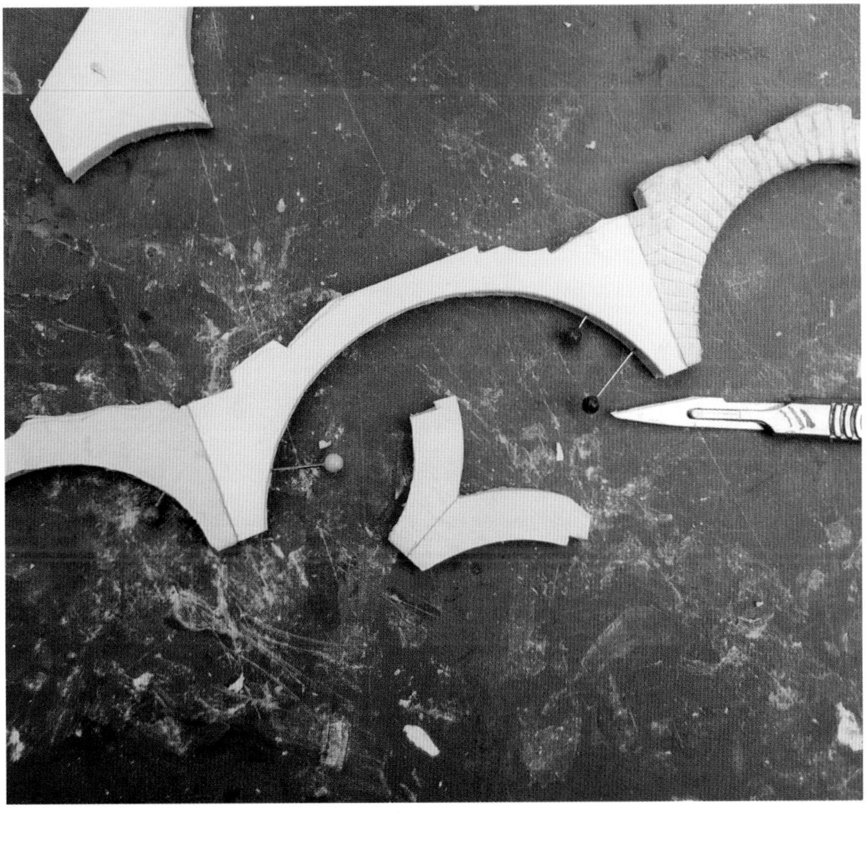

The arches have been cut out and fitted together. Note the irregular cuts to the top edge, all to add to the ruined appearance.

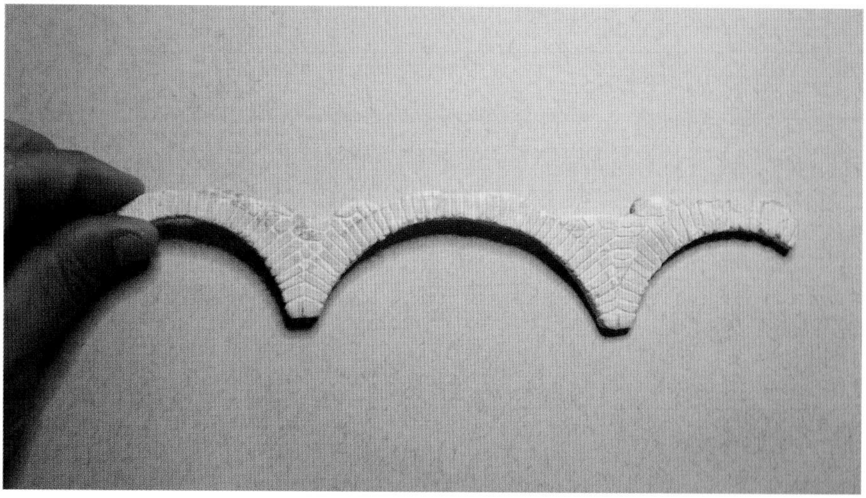

All the arch voussoirs have been scribed, along with the rubble stone infill.

All the arches have now been painted using the dry-brushing technique.

The supporting columns after painting. They have been 3D printed and were purchased from York Model Making. I used a combination of Humbrol and Halfords texture spray paint to give a realistic finish.

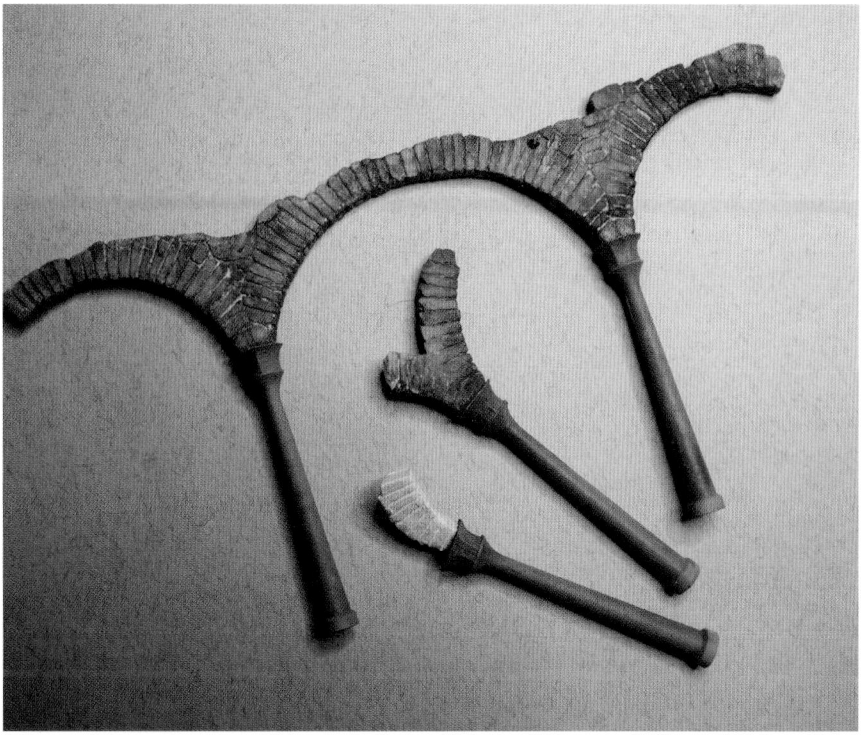

The finished columns attached to the full arches, and the remains of the arches.

The remains of the nave's arches have been fixed into position at the rear of the end wall.

FINISHING TOUCHES

The whole arch and the part arches were connected to the columns ready to be painted and weathered. All the masonry for the arches and for the window end wall of the abbey was painted with oil paint using techniques already explained. When the painting was completed, the nave window end wall, complete with the buttress on one side, was secured to the base. The four stone columns were also glued and fitted to the same base.

Once all the surviving ruins had been glued and secured, the base was grassed using static grass along with various pieces of flock to create rough scrub. To finish the ruins, ivy was draped and spray glued on to the broken side of the abbey's end wall, with it also creeping up some of the columns. I selected the scenic pack from Mini Natur, which gives a very good representation of this invasive plant. I also photographed various ivies growing on ruined structures to give me a good idea of how to position them on the model.

The abbey ruins located in the landscape of the diorama.

The abbey ruins blend nicely with all the landscaping.

As nature takes over, the scrub is visible, including ivy that is gradually creeping up the columns.

The final touching up of the ravine; this included adding more lichens to the rocks.

The entrance to the castle catacombs; access is from the pathway over the lower packhorse bridge.

All the rocks surrounding the castle towers and the ravine were first carved from insulation foam. The foam was then sealed with PVA, and coated with 'No More Cracks' plaster filler to give the rough surface texture required.

The finished results of the texturing after final painting. The remains of the curtain walls are visible behind.

THE GOTHIC ARCH FOLLY

With the model diorama now almost complete, I looked at what would further improve the scene. During my visit to Hawkstone Park I had photographed the Gothic arch folly. This artificial ruin stands as an eye catcher above the grotto, and because of this I decided it would be visually appealing and therefore worth adding to the diorama. Looking at the materials used for this structure I thought it would work as an addition to the castle curtain walls. The arch would then bridge the narrow-gauge railway, making an interesting feature.

The construction of this arch for a model follows almost exactly the steps explained earlier for the extension to Old John Folly. The arch was made slightly wider, taking into consideration the clearance needed for the trains to run through it. The folly was again made from two pieces of foam board glued together, marked and cut out, and covered with

The curtain wall extended as an archway over the railway. The reference for this came from Hawkstone Folly Park.

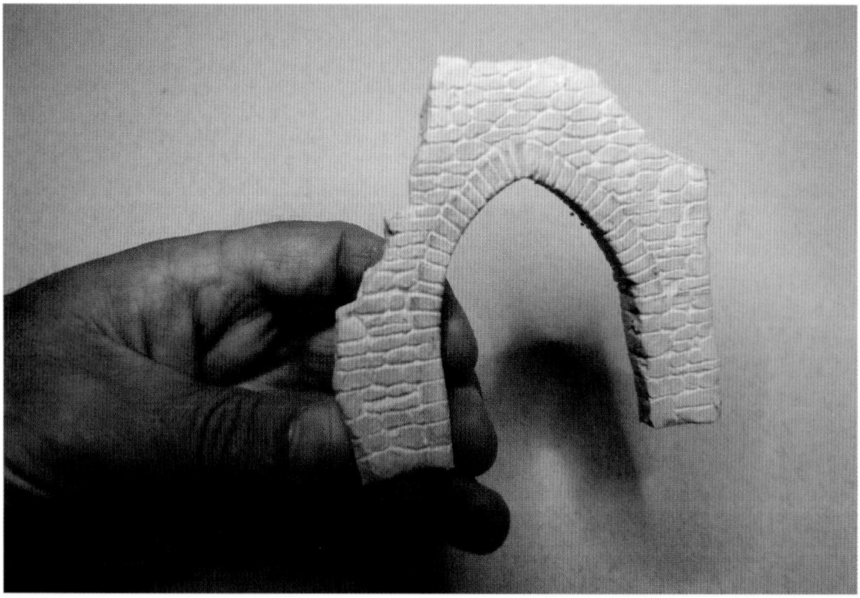

The archway, made from 6mm foam board. A large Gothic arch was cut out, along with the very irregular top ridge, all to add to the ruined appearance of the curtain walls. The structure has been covered with clay and scribed with rubble stone masonry.

Das modelling clay. Once all the stonework had been scribed and carved out, it was positioned to link up with the end of the curtain wall.

To make this link, a little extra work was required to continue the broken top, joining both together. A little Das was used for this, and some to fill the join on the facing side of the wall. When dry, the masonry was all scribed out to continue the walling over the join. Once painted and weathered, the arched folly looked as if it had always been a part of the curtain walling.

I found two resin castings of dragon heads topping stone pedestals; these were sold as park or garden statue features. I purchased both, supplied by A1 Models, at a model railway exhibition, and they made the perfect addition when placed each side of the arch, guarding its entrance and the tunnel beyond. Their natural resin colour wasn't too bad, but a coat of light buff-coloured spray paint improved the finish.

The left-hand corner where the arch was fitted needed more scenic work. This was first covered

The archway now fully painted and weathered, and ready to be located on the model.

The archway now located to connect with the curtain walling. I have added two dragon statues to stand guard at the entrance, all to enhance the fantasy theme of this model.

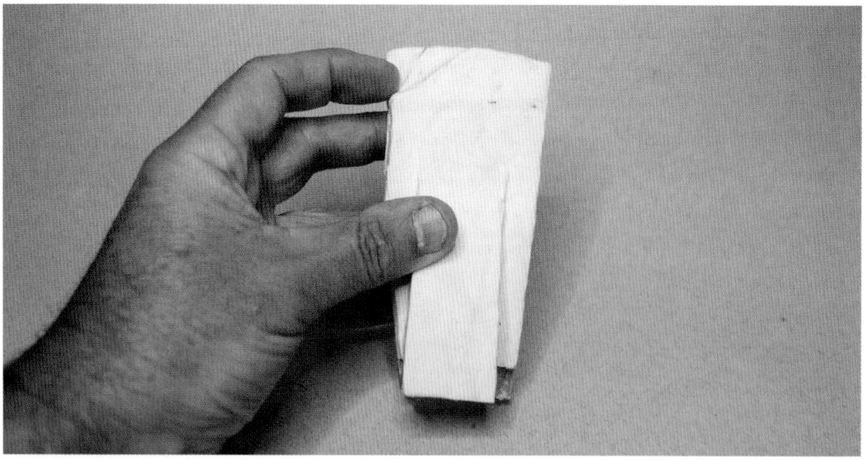

A section of curtain wall under construction. The wall was made up from 6mm foam board, with a facing supporting buttress made from mounting card.

The same section of curtain wall fixed into position between the two towers, finished and painted to match in. Ivy has been placed growing up in the corner of the wall, mainly to break up the expanse of the masonry.

with static grass with a good amount of Woodland Scenics flock added, especially around the base of the Gothic arch folly. The grassed area occupying the large part of the facing corner was enhanced by the addition of grass tuffs. These were obtained already made, as supplied by Mini Natur. While adding these on to the grassed areas I thought it might be a good idea to fix a few next to the side of the railway track, and even some smaller tufts between the rails. Adding small scenic features such as this can give those extra realistic touches to a model.

CREATING A BACKDROP

The final addition planned for this diorama was some kind of backdrop. This had to be complementary to what had been modelled in front of it, reflecting the overall fantasy theme. The backdrop would not have to be too deep, as the diorama was already a considerable depth. I eventually settled on a depth of 12 x 30in (305 x 762mm), which was the off-the-shelf size of a stretched canvas. This would give enough room to extend visually beyond the structures at the rear of the diorama.

With the format now sorted, I started to look for reference for a landscape that would fit the scene. I found a few by searching landscape galleries on the internet; however, the scene that really sparked my attention was 'The Old Man of Storr' on the Isle of Skye. The towering volcanic rock spires would fit in perfectly with the rest of the diorama. The scene also included the mountain ridges beyond the rock formations.

An option would have been to use a photographically produced backdrop, but this would have been expensive to produce and would not have given the right feel. I therefore decided to paint this scene direct on to the stretched canvas. Starting with the sky, this was painted using a wash of yellow ochre. While the paint was still wet, titanium white was added to create a glow in the sky, which was concentrated towards the centre of the canvas. When this had dried, I roughly painted in the mountains, starting with the skyline and then moving forwards and eventually painting in the spires of 'The Old Man of Storr'. Once I was happy with this I went over it, filling it in using a mix of paint made up from Payne's grey, mauve and titanium white.

The skyline was painted in first, adding more white to give the lightest shade of this mix. This mix was made darker as the mountain landscape became closer to the foreground. The rocky formations, including the tall spires, were all painted using the darkest shade. I used an angled chisel brush for this, as by using the side and the angled edge of the brush, a good representation of the rugged rocks was achieved reasonably easily.

The result at this stage gave the monochrome effect I was looking for; however, the rocks needed to be highlighted. This was achieved using titanium white mixed with a little yellow ochre to highlight just where the strong sunlight was catching them. Less was always more with this backdrop, and the secret was knowing when to stop. I was totally satisfied with the result; however, I thought the sky could be improved by adding dark clouds to highlight the yellow sunlight glow. Starting on the top edge of the canvas, this was painted using Payne's grey mixed with ultramarine blue, with more Payne's grey added at the edges to darken the effect.

The final result gave a much more dramatic sky, setting off this fantasy model to its best advantage. It is not always easy to produce a fitting backdrop to a model, but as long as it is not overdone and painted too brightly, it can always enhance the model placed in front of it. Always remember that the backdrop is there, not to take the viewer's eye away from the model in any way, but to give the visual illusion that the model continues. The trick is to make this blend almost seamlessly from the model in three dimensions to the backdrop in two dimensions.

Most modellers tend to shy away from attempting to paint a backdrop, possibly due to a lack of confidence. However, it is not as difficult as at first it might seem. (You can find out more about painting a complementary backdrop in *Creating Back Scenes*, also published by Crowood.)

ADDING SPECIAL EFFECTS AND DRESSINGS

The fantasy theme of this model diorama could always be added to in some way to make it more interesting to the viewer. The first way was to include some relative figures and creatures. My thinking here was to make up a cameo that would fit nicely into the fantasy-based theme. This led me to searching for scale figures and creatures at a local gaming shop called Spirit Games. I was lucky to find just what I was looking for in the way of a bearded wizard and a couple of dragons. The wizard came from the 'Dark Heaven Legends' range, available from Reaper Miniatures. The 'Young Fire Dragon' came from the 'Dark Heaven Bones' range. The 'Nachtlufte' dragon was from the 'Dark Heaven Apocalypse' range, again from the American game suppliers Reaper Miniatures.

All these models would require painting, with the white metal models prepared with an acrylic primer applied first. I used the new range of acrylic paints from Omen Miniatures for the wizard, which I found to be ideal due to their quick drying properties. The paints are also ready mixed to authentic colours for figure painting, including flesh tones. The dragons,

One of the dragons lacking its wings supplied in the 'Dark Heaven' range from Reaper Miniatures. A dragon such as this would be ideal to dress this fantasy model.

The right-hand side of the diorama dressed out with a dragon being confronted by a well-known fantasy wizard, both fully painted and positioned on the model to create a believable cameo action scene.

The dragon, flexing its wings as it emerges from its lair in the caves.

however, were painted with artist's oil paints allowing for drying times in between each coat.

The Young Fire Dragon was placed at the entrance to the larger of the caves, the cave being the creature's lair. I set the bearded wizard on the steps in front of the cave, with him confronting the dragon with a staff. The inspiration for this setting came from the trilogy of films based on a famous series of novels by J. R. R. Tolkien. The larger dragon will be placed on top of the highest ruined castle tower flexing its wings. At the time of writing this has not yet been completed.

CREATING SPECIAL EFFECTS

To add further to the fantasy, I wanted to create some special effects. My thinking was first to try and produce a mist rising from the bottom of the waterfall: if this could be fitted in the right position it should create an authentic atmosphere, therefore adding another dimension to the model. The search was now on to find a mister unit that would give me the right effect. I eventually saw a sample mood light under the model name of 'Liv USB Aroma Diffuser'. This light, made by Zen, has a reservoir that is filled with water; this is heated from underneath, creating a controlled flow of mist, which is emitted from the outlet. The unit is powered using a mains USB adapter with a USB cable, connected to the unit by a DS jack.

The main problem with a unit such as this is its size, as it measures 3.5in (89mm) in diameter by 3in (76mm) deep, and it would require a space big enough for it to fit directly underneath the model. Therefore to accommodate the unit a sub-base was needed, to raise the baseboard at least 3in (76mm). I made this up using MDF cut to this depth and then constructed to the outer measurements of the baseboard, and using 1 x 1in (25 x 25mm) timber battens on the corners.

A small hole was then drilled through the baseboard to line up exactly at the bottom of the waterfall, with a rock placed in front to mask the hole from view. The unit could then be positioned with the mist outlet directly underneath the drilled hole. If positioned correctly the mist should rise gradually from the unit's outlet, through the hole and continue rising within the cliff faces of the ravine.

This effect worked very well, and it was well worth the time, expense and effort to install this unit. There are other mister units on the market that would work as well. I have seen similar units available

The three bridges are the centrepiece to this diorama, all spanning the deep ravine with its cascading waterfall. I intend to install a mister, which will create an atmospheric, mystical feel to the model.

The finished diorama with the narrow-gauge train crossing the bridge over 'Raven's Ravine'.

from garden centres that are made to be combined with inside water features. One word of warning, however: some of these units can emit the mist too fast, which will look out of place on a scale model. If a more dramatic effect is desired, this could be worth looking at, especially if you are trying to create, say, volcanic vent action or something similar.

At the time of writing this book, this is the only special effect added to the diorama, but I would like to add a few others in the future, and in particular look at how different lighting might enhance this model.

One idea was to have a lighting rig positioned above the front of the diorama. The rig would consist of a few rows of LEDs, possibly with one orange row, one red row, one blue row and one emitting bright white light. These would need to be wired and connected to some kind of control unit available to create a number of different lighting effects. It would be a good idea if the lights could be made to flash on and off, strobe, or fade between colours.

I am no electrician and will be the first to admit it, so professional assistance from someone who knows what they are doing will be appreciated when it comes to building the rig. It was suggested that an appropriate set of Christmas tree lights might be an option to give the desired effects, and this is definitely worth considering.

To conclude, I hope that the building of this fantasy-themed diorama layout has given inspiration to anyone reading this book. I don't expect everyone to try and build a replica of 'Raven's Ravine', but I hope that by describing the techniques I have used, they will be beneficial to most modellers. I would also like to think that by reading this chapter, it will show that model making does not have to be taken too seriously. It is a hobby, at the end of the day, and you should have fun taking part. I know that I had fun building 'Raven's Ravine', and since exhibiting the model at recent exhibitions, I have been overwhelmed by the positive response from the visiting public.

CHAPTER SIX

CREATING THE SETTING FOR IMAGINARY BUILDINGS AND STRUCTURES

When it comes to providing the setting in which to position our imaginary buildings and structures, it is well worth taking a look at the works of the contemporary master artists of the late eighteenth and early nineteenth centuries. In this period a school of artists came to prominence where in landscape painting the emphasis was towards the more romantic rather than actual true life.

This movement and style of art was known more commonly as the 'Picturesque Movement'. Talented artists would tend to exaggerate the land forms and features, using their technical ability to reproduce light and shade to their advantage, thus forming a convincing but much more romantic image. This approach to painting soon became very fashionable with the public of the time.

Painters often would favour buildings or structures in ruin, as these could be portrayed against a dramatic stormy or moonlit sky. Ruins would be presented with ivy growth creeping over them, usually standing on jagged rock formations, in a rather grotesque portrayal. The ruined remains of the great abbeys were always a favourite, where architecture would blend dramatically with land-

A surreal image of spindly birch trees on Stanton Moor in Derbyshire. This very eerie landscape could be modelled, especially if special effects were added such as selected lighting and mist-emitting units.

The dramatic and mystical rock formations at Beacon Hill, which looks even more sinister because it is in silhouette. This effect could be reproduced on a model diorama by back lighting through a semi-transparent material used for the backdrop.

scape. Another favourite would be an overgrown graveyard or secret walled garden. The graveyard can be modelled featuring unmaintained gravestones, tombs and larger mausoleums built to resemble majestic classical temples.

This type of imagery has been revived in the movie industry, from early horror films through to the more recent well known fantasy movies. The creation of many film sets and miniatures has been influenced by the work of the 'Picturesque Movement' from the past.

It is appropriate that the hobby of model making follows the same influences, and it is well worth considering presenting our imaginary buildings or structures in the same way. Although we strive to create our models as accurately as possible to real life, there is always room for a little artistic licence to give them more visual appeal.

In the previous chapter I tried to use some of these influences to create a small table-top model railway. I purposely used extreme terrain, together with the exaggerated positioning of the structures, to give a more interesting visual impact to the diorama – this will work as long as we are not tempted to load the diorama without any thought as to how structures will balance with each other. If this is not properly addressed, the final appearance will not look convincing at all. If you are not sure how this balance will finally look, it will be well worth making simple mock-ups of all the structures first; these can be moved around until pleasing and convincing results are obtained.

SELECTING PROTOTYPE LANDSCAPE FEATURES

There are many natural landscape features that can be selected to set off our models to the best of their advantage. In the UK alone we have some very dramatic rock formations, which would easily complement the more fantasy miniature structures. Some of these rock formations have been used to

The industrial ruins at Lums Dale, near to Matlock. Nature is now taking over the whole scene. This can easily be replicated by using the vast amount of scenic materials now available.

A group of dead trees in a flooded marl pit. This could make another eerie-looking cameo scene or setting for a sinister-looking imaginary structure.

Another photograph of the same scene. By selecting a few dead twigs and setting them into a surface coated in layers of clear varnish to represent the water, a model could be made of this interesting scene. If the right lighting and mist were also added it could be transformed into a primitive and savage-looking landscape.

set off structures in the past by landowners. The ones that instantly come to mind are follies such as Mow Cop or Tregeagle's Dilemma, the latter being a fifteenth-century chapel crowning an impressive outcrop of rock near to Roche in Cornwall.

Unusual rock strata, however, is not the only form of landscape or terrain to consider. Moorland and boggy ground can be an interesting alternative, and if you include some dead trees, the landscape can look quite sinister. Putting a ruined structure within this mysterious marshland setting will play on the viewer's imagination and evoke a land that is haunted by demons.

Trees can always add this element of mystery, especially if they are old or dead, or if one stands alone and is bent into a curious shape by the strong prevailing winds. Trees in these situations can take on weird shapes, like witches' broomsticks or demons' fingers. As modellers we should always be on the lookout for such interesting prototypes within the natural world. Always carry a camera with you to record what you may come across.

I found a perfect location with a group of dead trees standing within a flooded gravel or marl pit only a mile or so from my home. I must have passed the location hundreds of times without taking any notice. Since starting to write this book, however, I took a closer look and was inspired to try and recreate the scene in miniature one day. I have included in the book reference photographs taken at the site, as it

Any structure with Gothic arches can look good on a model. This simple stone shelter in Stapenhill Gardens has been definitely enhanced by providing it with the two Gothic arches.

Bridges, especially those of primitive origin, can add special interest to a model diorama. This is the Washgate packhorse bridge crossing the upper River Dove, and was my prototype inspiration for the sweeping arched bridge crossing 'Raven's Ravine'.

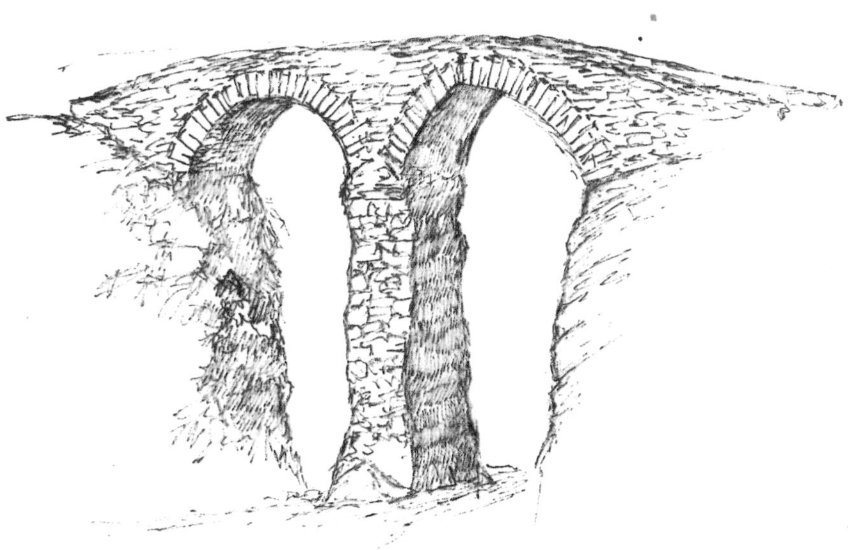

A drawing I made during the planning of 'Raven's Ravine'. It features the packhorse bridge found at Wycoller: I have simply extended the central pier, which adds to the primitive appearance of this interesting structure.

would definitely be worth considering for a setting for a future fantasy model featuring a ruined building or structure.

In the previous chapter I wanted to include a few dramatic rock formations for the 'Raven's Ravine' diorama. I was able to find prototype reference in two main locations. For the ravine, I found the perfect prototype in mid-Shropshire at Hawkstone Park. This forgotten park, along with the ruins of the medieval Red Castle, stands within a high ridge of sandstone, which has evoked romantic impressions and images of Arthurian legends.

The natural landscape was recognized and skilfully enhanced by the Hill family in the eighteenth and nineteenth centuries. The Hills used the natural rock formations to create man-made caves and grottos, and a number of follies were also constructed. The park was a forgotten masterpiece until this natural landscape gem was brought back to life under a restoration programme in 1990.

Since then the park has seen the follies and underground grottos restored and opened for the general public to experience this spectacular landscape. It is hoped in the future that the ruined towers of Red Castle will be included under this restoration plan, providing the perfect highlight to the park, especially with its historical association with the knights of King Arthur. However, until this happens to the prototype,

Cameo scenes such as this one at Buckfastleigh old church creates a view through to a focal point. This is made more visually interesting because the archway we are looking through is in a ruined form. It is always worth considering cameo scenes such as this to add to a model.

The ruins of Buckfastleigh church again, which could provide another surreal cameo scene to be modelled.

One of the ancient crosses found on the vast remoteness of Dartmoor. They are thought to be navigational beacons, to guide priests who were crossing the moor. A structure such as this would create an interesting focal point on a model diorama.

Gravestones and memorials can make interesting subjects for models.

The large tombhead in Stapenhill Cemetery would make a super cameo scene on a model diorama. The interesting shape, together with the supporting columns at the front, make the structure almost temple-like in appearance.

A closer view of the same tomb to show the detail. The ivy growth creeping up the right-hand side would also be worth adding to such a model.

The remains of the old church in Ticknall, south Derbyshire. This ruin would definitely create a surreal feel to a cameo-modelled scene, which could be added to the concept model presented in the next few images. This could be made even more eerie by combining the ruin with mist drifting across the scene, which, with the aid of special effects, would be achievable in model form.

I decided to include the ruined towers of Red Castle in miniature on the 'Raven's Ravine' diorama, the construction of which, along with the dramatic terrain found at Hawkstone Park, was explained in detail in the last chapter.

SPECIAL EFFECTS

We can now add a different dimension as well as just creating the physical elements to our model railways, or dioramas. This would be especially appropriate in the case of the more fantasy settings for our models.

All the physical elements, such as the buildings, structures and dramatic landscape, would be enhanced greatly by adding some special effects. These could be added as visual effects or even added as sound effects. In this digital world these are more available to the modeller than in the past. The other advantage is that they can be produced as microchip units, which make them easy to install or hide within a model. The other advantage is that some of these devices can be operated from a laptop computer or even possibly a smart phone.

The only issue I have is when the special effects are overdone; this is especially true when it comes to some model railways at exhibitions.

At the exhibitions, I have seen, or should I say, heard so many conflicting sounds emitted, together with sound effects that are set far too loud for the scale of the layouts. This is very off-putting, and will only result in creating a nuisance to anyone who happens to be in the close vicinity. This can be very annoying, especially when it is going on all day at an exhibition. I am not against adding sound effects, far from it, so long as they are emitted at the right level and with consideration to others. In my opinion some of the sounds of the locomotives are far too loud and over used, and should be toned down to a more subtle and realistic level. Remember, the models we are displaying are scaled right down, and therefore the sound emitting from them should be scaled down as well.

This applies to other sounds that might be part of a model railway layout or a diorama, whether they are part of an urban or a rural environment. In urban towns or cities we are more familiar with emergency sirens or alarm systems going off, piercing the subdued everyday sounds. In the country, however, these sounds are a rarity, and we are more

A flat plan to create a model railway layout devoted to a famous boy wizard.

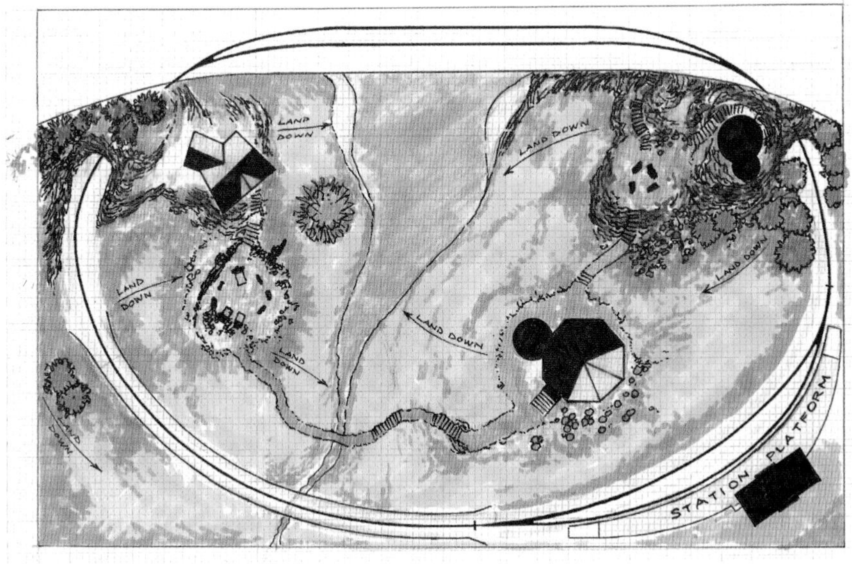

One stage further from the flat plan: a three-dimensional visualization of what the model would look like. I have included a selection of structures and cameo scenes that would be built in model form. The castle, however, due to its size, features on the painted backdrop.

My own illustration of this eerie-looking structure, to show it in more detail. On the model it appears beyond the haunted graveyard. This timber-clad, decaying shack-like building could be constructed from scrapwood. The framework could be made up from spent rocket sticks, and the cladding from coffee stirrers or old wood veneers.

Ornate Celtic crosses such as this one at Stapenhill Cemetery can make an interesting focal point on a model.

This headstone is another interesting shape to model.

Closer view of the same cross as above. The name here made me smile!

familiar with the more pastoral sounds made by the animals in the fields or in the farmyard. This ambient sound might be interrupted by a tractor starting up, or heard ploughing a field. Bird sounds are also heard more in the country than in the town, such as the distinctive call of a cock pheasant in the fields to a cockerel crowing in the farmyard. These sounds need to follow the same rule, however, and should be scaled down in tone to fit into their miniature environment.

Besides creating authentic sound effects for a model railway or diorama, other special effects can be added.

The impressive gateway to the cemetery at Stapenhill. The Gothic architecture, which includes arches, gables and spires, would make a super model, perhaps using the centre section to create a decorative tunnel mouth on a fantasy-themed model railway.

This interesting monolith carved from wood stands on the monastic washlands near to Burton Abbey. Again, this would create a focal point to a cameo-modelled scene. The scrubland surrounding it is also worth considering.

The unusual shaped window within the walls of Codnor Castle, a feature that could be included in a cameo ruin scene.

Illustration of the impressive 'Bomb Rocks', as I was not allowed to photograph them. The volcanic rocks are Pre-Cambrian, and date from 600 million years ago. They are found on land near to Charnwood Lodge, which is not far from the rock formations at Beacon Hill. They would make a perfect addition to a modelled primitive landscape.

I made these sketches when planning 'Raven's Ravine'. They show how ruins can enhance or blend in with extreme terrain modelling. One of the sketches depicts the volcanic panicles of 'The Old Man of Storr' on the Isle of Skye. This features on the backdrop for 'Raven's Ravine', as it complements the model in front of it perfectly.

The volcanic rocky crag topped with the castle-like folly of 'Mow Cop'. This is crying out to feature on a model layout or diorama.

The arches leading from the cloister to the Chapter House within the ruins of Wenlock Priory. Again, these could be incorporated into a model diorama. They are not unlike the arches I modelled for the abbey on 'Raven's Ravine'.

RIGHT: ***The white card concept model of the castle that I photographed on a studio tour. It just shows the attention to detail shown to model making within the film industry.***

BELOW: ***The finished model, photographed while visiting 'Leavesden Studios'. The model is a truly magnificent piece of work and certainly took my breath away. I would recommend that anyone interested in miniatures or model making visits the studios: you won't be disappointed.***

Authentic street lighting, arc lighting of a welding torch or a smouldering bonfire are favourites for model railways. However, for a fantasy model layout or diorama we can be a little more adventurous.

I intend to add some special visual effects to the project model of 'Raven's Ravine', although careful attention will always be made not to overdo these. My first thoughts were towards adding a mist rising from the bottom of the waterfall at the base of the ravine. If a special effects unit were concealed underneath, the mist produced could be controlled to rise in the right place. The main objective would be to make this effect appear to be as realistic as possible. How this was achieved for the project was covered in the last chapter. Further lighting and sound effects will be added at some time in the future; hopefully, adding these extra dimensions to this model will make it more attractive to the viewing public.

APPENDIX: COLOUR MIXING GUIDE

This guide has been produced to help modellers achieve realistic colours when it comes to the painting stage of most model-making projects. I have purposely shown how colour can be mixed, starting from a basic range of artist's oil paints. These are available in tubes, and can be mixed easily to create a vast range of other colours and shades. The colours I have used have been specially selected to be used when trying to replicate materials used for buildings and structures, together with colours seen in the natural terrain and landscape.

Prototype reference: light green lichens on rocks.

Prototype reference: yellow lichens growing on rocks.

Prototype reference: sun-bleached and silvered timbers.

Prototype reference: green and yellow lichens on rock faces.

Prototype reference: sandstone walling.

Prototype reference: well worn brickwork.

Prototype reference: rusting and weathered corrugated metal sheeting.

Prototype reference: duck weed on the surface of water.

Prototype reference: more weathered brickwork.

Prototype reference: random stone masonry.

Prototype reference: random cobbles in a yard.

Prototype reference: mosses and lichens growing on a tiled roof.

Prototype reference: well worn and silvered woodwork.

Colours direct from the tube (left to right): yellow ochre, titanium white, Payne's grey.

Colour mix: yellow ochre + titanium white. Use for: sandstone, (Cotswold) limestone, lichens on rocks, stone, brickwork and roofs.
Colour mix: yellow ochre + Payne's grey. Use for: gritstone, tree trunks and branches, cobbles, treated timber, old thatch.

Colour mix: yellow ochre + Payne's grey + titanium white. Use for: sandstone, limestone, concrete, paving slabs, cobbles.

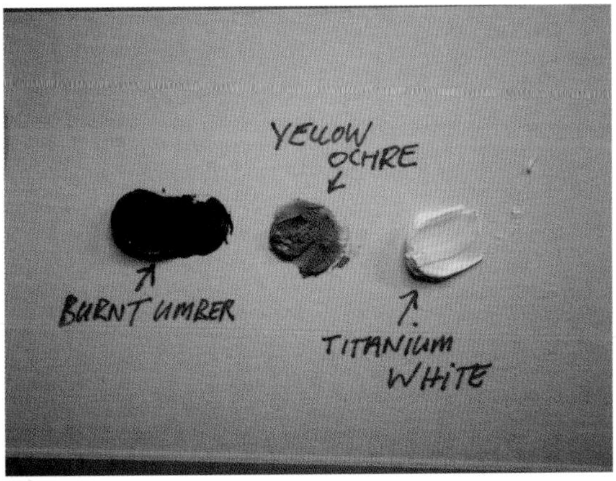

Colours direct from the tube: burnt umber, yellow ochre and titanium white.

Colour mix: burnt umber + yellow ochre. Use for: gritstone, granite, treated timber, cobbles, dark flesh tones.
Colour mix: burnt umber + yellow ochre + titanium white. Use for: gritstone, shales, concrete, cobbles, weathered timber and old worn thatch.

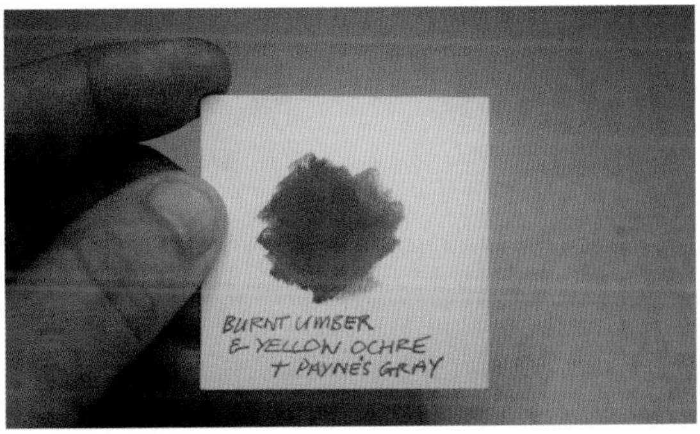

Colour mix: burnt umber + yellow ochre + Payne's grey.
Use for: limestone, shales, slate, weathered and silvered timber, beech tree trunks and branches, old worn thatch.

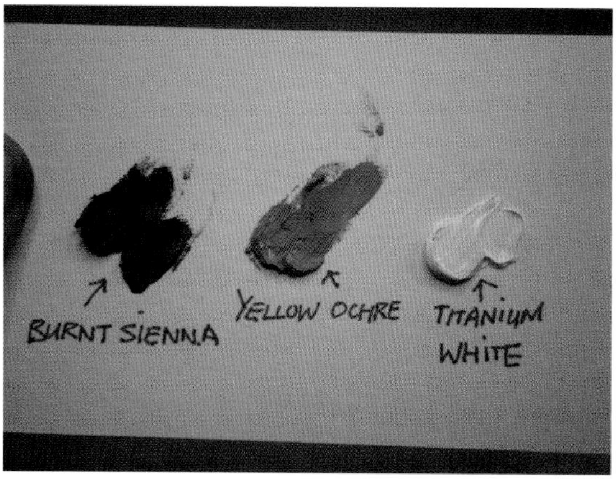

Colours direct from the tube (left to right): burnt sienna, yellow ochre and titanium white.

Colour mix: burnt sienna + yellow ochre. Use for: burnt worn brick, gritstone, dark sandstone, dark terracotta tiles.
Colour mix: burnt sienna + yellow ochre + titanium white. Use for: sandstone, light weathered and worn brick, light weathered terracotta tiles.

Colour mix: burnt umber + yellow ochre + Payne's grey. Use for: gritstone, dark slate, shales, dark timber and coniferous tree bark.

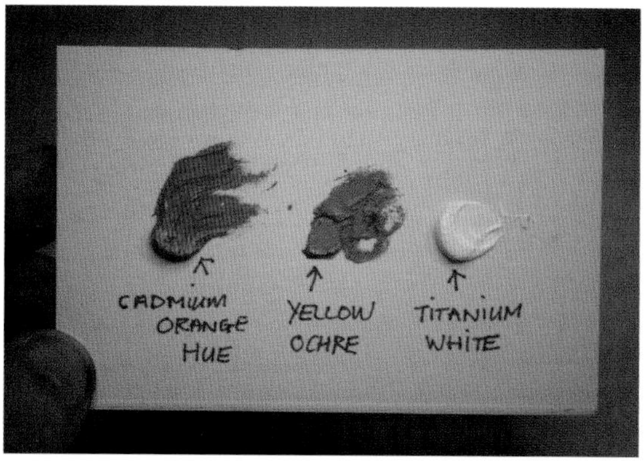

Colours direct from the tube (left to right): cadmium orange (hue), yellow ochre, titanium white.

Colour mix: cadmium orange (hue) + yellow ochre. Use for: light weathered brickwork, terracotta tiles, sand, sandstone, rust, flesh tones.

Colour mix: cadmium orange (hue) + yellow ochre + titanium white. Use for: light sandstone, sand, light weathered brickwork, light terracotta tiles, flesh tones.

Colour mix: cadmium orange (hue) + titanium white. Use for: light weathered brickwork, light terracotta tiles, flesh tones.

Colour mix: cadmium orange (hue) + Payne's grey. Use for: dark sandstone, gritstone, dark weathered brickwork, cobbles, dark flesh tones.

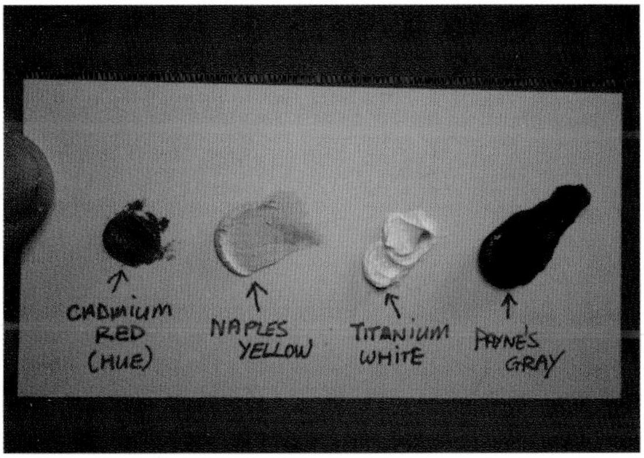

Colours direct from the tube (left to right): cadmium red (hue), Naples yellow, titanium white, Payne's grey.

Colour mix: cadmium red + Naples yellow. Use for: new and engineering brickwork, rust and rusting metal, terracotta tiles.
Colour mix: cadmium red + titanium white. Use for: light brickwork, light terracotta tiles.
Colour mix: cadmium red + Payne's grey. Use for: dark brickwork, dark terracotta tiles.

Colours direct from the tube: terre verte (hue) + yellow ochre + titanium white.

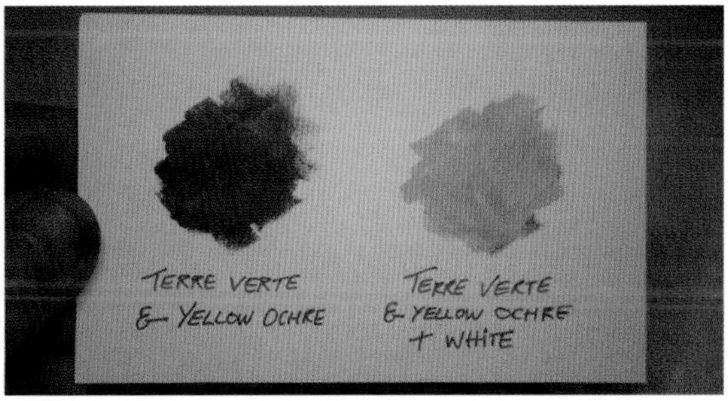

Colour mix: terre verte (hue) + yellow ochre. Use for: mosses, algae on stone, rocks and brickwork, grasses, scrub, foliage.
Colour mix: terre verte (hue) + yellow ochre + titanium white. Use for: lichens on rocks, tiled and slate roofs, weathered timbers, bark of silver birch trees.

Colour mix: terre verte (hue) + yellow ochre + Payne's grey. Use for: slate, slate roofs, shales, granite, dark weathered timber.
Colour mix: terre verte (hue) + chrome yellow + titanium white. Use for: lichens on rocks, tiled and slate roofs, light grasses and sedges, foliage, algae growth on trees and timber, duck weed on water, reeds and rushes.

Colours from the tube: sap green, chrome yellow, titanium white.

Colour mix: sap green + chrome yellow. Use for: spring grass, spring foliage, scrub and weeds.
Colour mix: sap green + chrome yellow + titanium white. Use for: lichens on rocks, walls and roofs, light grasses and sedges, dead grasses.
Colour mix: sap green + yellow ochre. Use for: lichens on rocks, walls and roofs, dead grass, straw, new thatch.

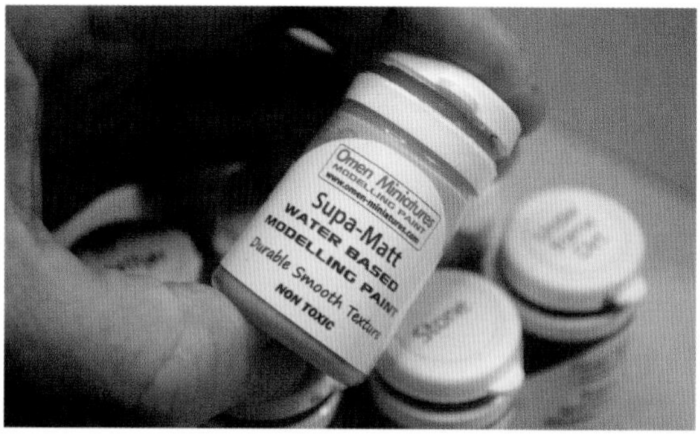

One of the new paints from 'Omen Miniatures'. They are quick drying with a super matt finish, available in 18mm pots, and have been specially mixed to create a range of colours with the model maker in mind. I have found them perfect to use for figure painting, and where a flat colour needs to be applied.

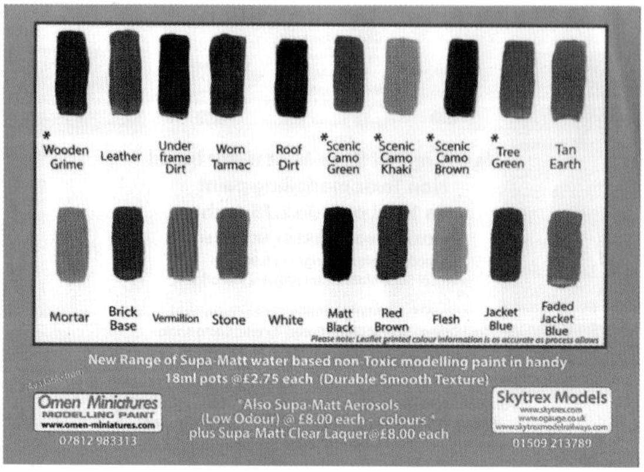

LEFT: I have included a colour chart of the colours available in this range, for modellers to use direct from the pot.

SUPPLIERS OF EQUIPMENT AND MATERIALS

Air Framed
25 Wilmot Drive, Smalley, Ilkeston, Derbyshire, DE7 6EL
Telephone: 07971 741478 and 01332 781795
Email: nigel@airframed.co.uk
www.airframed.co.uk
Bespoke glass display cases

Dapol Models
Gledrid Industrial Park, Chirk, Wrexham, LL14 5DG
Telephone: 0169 1774455
www.dapol.co.uk
Building kits, off-the-shelf models and accessories

Dart Castings & Shire Scenes
17 Hurst Close, Staplehurst, Tonbridge Wells, Kent, TN12 0BX
Telephone: 01580 892917
www.dartcastings.co.uk

Double O Scenics
33 Willis Road, Haddenham, Buckinghamshire, HP17 8HL
www.doubleoscenics.weebly.com

Dovedale Models by David Wright
6 Ivy Court, Hilton, Derbyshire, DE65 5WD
Telephone: 01283 733547
david@dovedalemodels.co.uk
Bespoke model-making services and scenic modelling DVDs

Duncan Models
34 Waters Road, Salisbury, Wiltshire, SP1 3NX
Telephone: 01722 321041
www.duncanmodels.co.uk

Eileen's Emporium
Unit 19, 12 Higham Business Centre, Newent Road, Gloucester, GL2 8DN
Telephone: 01531 828009
www.eileensemporium.com

Evergreen Scale Models, Inc.
12808 NE 125th Way, Kirkland, WA 98034, USA

Freestone Models
28 Newland Mill, Whitney, Oxfordshire, OX28 3HH
Telephone: 01993 775975
www.freestonemodels.co.uk
Foam board, Das modelling clay, paints, brushes, card and styrene

Green Scene
60 Hollymount, Worcester, WR4 9SF
http://green-scene.co.uk
Email: greenscenes@btopenworld.com

Heki–Flor
HEKI-Kittler GmbH, Modellbahnzubehor D-76437 Rastatt

Hobby Holidays
The Spinney, Low Street, Beckingham, Nr. Doncaster, South Yorkshire, DN10 4PW
Telephone: 01427 848979
www.hobbyholidays.co.uk

Invertrain Model Railways Heroes of the Footplate (Whitby Fisher Folk)
33 Rose Gardens, Cairney hill, Dunfermline, KY12 8QS
www.invertrain.com

Jackson's Art Suppliers
1 Farleigh Place,
London, N16 7SX
Telephone: 020 7254 0077
www.jacksonsart.com

Langley Models
166 Three Bridges Road, Crawley, Sussex, RH10 1LH

Telephone: 0870 0660 416
www.langleymodels.co.uk

Metcalfe Models
Bell Busk, Skipton, North Yorkshire, BD23 4DU

Natural Scenics Ltd
Unit 7, Ashley Industrial Estate,
Mereside, Soham, Cambridgeshire, CB7 5EE
Telephone: 01353 721888
Email: info@naturalscenics.co.uk
www.naturalscenics.co.uk

Omen Miniatures
Telephone: 07812 983313
www.omen-miniatures.com
Miniature figure range and modelling paint

PLM Cast-A-Ways
12 New Street, Merryhill, Wolverhampton, WV3 7NW
Telephone: 01902 570810
Mobile: 07930 049338

Reaper Miniatures
Dark Heaven Legends
www.reapermini.com

S & D Models
Highbridge Works, PO Box 101, Burnham-on-Sea, TA9 4WA
www.sanddmodels.co.uk

'Scenecraft' by Bachmann
Bachmann Europe plc
www.bachmann.co.uk

Skaledale by Hornby
Hornby Hobbies Ltd., Westwood, Margate, Kent, CT9 4JX
www.expressmodels.co.uk
Email: sales@expressmodels.co.uk
www.hornby.com

Skytrex 2013
Skytrex 2013, 1, Charnwood Business Park,
North Road, Loughborough, Leicestershire,
LE11 1LE (order line: 01509 213789)
www.ogauge.com

Slater's (Platikard) Ltd
Old Road, Darley Dale, Matlock, Derbyshire, DE4 2ER
Telephone: 01629 734053
https://Slatersplastikard.com

Springside Models
2 Springside Cottages, Dornafield Road, Ipplepen, Newton Abbot, Devon, TQ12 5SJ
Telephone: 01803 813749
www.springsidemodels.com

Squires Model & Craft Tools
100 London Road, Bognor Regis, West Sussex, PO21 1DD
Telephone: 01243 842424
www.squirestools.com
Scale rules, small squares, scalpels, blades, cutting mats, paint brushes, evergreen styrene stripsheet and general tools

The Model Tree Shop
Telephone: 01890 819021
Email: steve@themodeltreeshop.co.uk

Warhammer Derby
42, Sadler Gate, Derby DE1 3NR
Telephone: 01332 371657

Woodland Scenics
PO Box 98, Linn Creek, MO 65052, USA
Scenic materials, accessories, figures and dressings

York Model Making
Unit 13, Bull Centre, Stockton-on-the-Forest, York, YO32 9LE
www.yorkmodelmaking.co.uk

PLACES OF INTEREST TO VISIT

Avoncroft Museum
Stoke Heath, Bromsgrove,
Worcestershire, B60 4JR
Telephone: 01527 831363 / 831886
www.avoncroft.org.uk

Bolton Abbey
Estate Office,
Bolton Abbey,
Skipton,
North Yorkshire, BD23 6EX
Telephone: 01756 718009
www.boltonabbey.com

Clun Castle
Visitor Information Centre and Museum
Telephone: 01588 640541
www.clunmuseum.org.uk
www.shropshirehistory.org.uk

Codnor Castle
Codnor Castle Heritage Trust
Codnor, near Ripley, Derbyshire
www.codnorcastle.co.uk

Daniels Mill Trust
Eardington,
Bridgenorth,
Shropshire, WV16 5JL
Telephone: 01746 762753
www.danielsmill.co.uk

Glastonbury Abbey
The Abbey Gatehouse, Magdalene Street,
Glastonbury, Somerset, BA6 9EL
Email: info@glastonburyabbey.com
education@glastonburyabbey.com
www.glastonburyabbey.com
English Heritage
Tel: 0370 333 1181

Hawkstone Park Follies
Weston-Under-Redcastle,
Shrewsbury, Shropshire, SY4 5JY
Email: follies@hawkstone.co.uk
www.hawkstoneparkfollies.co.uk

Heage Windmill
Chesterfield Road,
Heage, Belper,
Derbyshire, DE56 2BH
Telephone: 01773 853579
www.heagewindmill.org.uk

Miniature World
High Street,
Bourton-on-the-Water,
Gloucestershire, GL54 2AQ
Telephone: 01451 810121

National Trust
Bridge Cottage,
Flatford Mill,
East Bergholt, Nr Ipswich,
Suffolk, CO7 6UL
Telephone: 01206 298260

Pendon Museum
Long Wittenham, Abingdon,
Oxfordshire, OX14 4QD
Telephone: 01865 407365
www.pendonmuseum.com

Peveril Castle
Castleton Tourist Office,
Castle Street,
Castleton,
Derbyshire, S30 2WG
Telephone: 01629 813227

Sinai Park House
Guided Tours
Telephone: Kate Murphy on 01283 544161 or 01889 598600

Skipton Castle
North Yorkshire, BD23 1AW
Telephone: 01756 792442
www.skiptoncastle.co.uk

St Fagans National History Museum
Cardiff, South Wales, CF56XB
Telephone: 029 20573500

Stokesay Castle
Craven Arms,
Shropshire, SY7 9AH.
Telephone: 01588 672544
English-heritage.org.uk/stokesaycastle

Thaxted Windmill
Thaxted Information Centre
Telephone: 01371 831641
www.thaxted.co.uk

The Old Mill
Mill Lane,
Lower Slaughter,
Gloucestershire, GL54 2HX
Telephone: 01451 820052
www.oldmill-lowerslaughter.com

Tutbury Castle
Tutbury,
Staffordshire, DE13 9JF
Telephone: 01283 812129
www.tutburycastle.com

Warner Bros Studio Tour London
The Making of Harry Potter
Leavesden Studios, Nr Watford, Hertfordshire

FURTHER READING

Bryan, Anthony *Windmills & Watermills – Photographic Memories* (The Frith Book Company)
Constable, John *Landscapes in Miniature* (The Lutterworth Press, Guildford, and Sheldon Press, London)
Gravett, Gordon *Modelling Grassland and Landscape Detailing* (Wild Swan Publications)
Gravett, Gordon *Modelling Trees – Part One – Broadleaf Trees* (Wild Swan Publications)
Sunshine, Paula *Wattle and Daub* (Shire Library)
Viner, David *Wagons and Carts* (Shire Library)
Yorke, Trevor *British Architectural Styles – An Easy Reference Guide* (Countryside Books, Newbury)

INDEX